OUR ZOO

When George Mottershead moved to the village of Upton-by-Chester in 1930 to realise his dream of opening a zoo without bars, his four-year-old daughter June had no idea how extraordinary her life would become. Soon her best friend was a chimpanzee called Mary, lion cubs and parrots were vying for her attention in the kitchen, and finding a bear tucked up in bed was no more unusual than talking to a tapir about Granny's lemon curd. Pelican, penguin or polar bear – for June they were simply family.

OUR ZOO

OUR ZOO

by

June Mottershead
with Penelope Dening

Magna Large Print Books
Long Preston, North Yorkshire,
BD23 4ND, England.

British Library Cataloguing in Publication Data.

Mottershead, June with Dening, Penelope
    Our zoo.

A catalogue record of this book is
available from the British Library

ISBN   978-0-7505-4155-8

First published in Great Britain in 2014 by
Headline Publishing Group

Copyright © 2014 Big Talk Productions Limited

Cover illustration © mirrorpix

Published in Large Print 2015 by arrangement with
Headline Publishing Group Ltd.

Magna Large Print is an imprint of Library Magna Books Ltd.

Printed and bound in Great Britain by
T.J. (International) Ltd., Cornwall, PL28 8RW

Dedicated to the memory of
Fred Williams
1925–2012

Chester Zoo in 1931

(Years of later deve[lopment]
shown in bracke[ts])

1 – Llamas (1937)
2 – Peter & Lion (1942)
3 – Children's Play Area (1937)
4 – Indoor Lion Pen (1937)
5 – Original Lion Pen Archway
6 – Site for Outdoor Lion Enclosure
   (foundation stone laid 1937,
   building delayed until 1947)
7 – Griffon Vultures
8 – Mandrills & Leopards
9 – Penguins
10 – Tapir (1932)
11 – Malayan Bear (1937)
12 – Café
13 – Aquarium
14 – Elephants (1941)
15 – Bird Aviary
16 – Canadian Black Bears (Adam & Eve)
17 – Rhesus Monkeys
18 – Tourico Aviary
19 – Pelicans
20 – Pheasant Aviary
21 – Conservatory
   Crocodiles, Snakes, & Tropical Finches
22 – Chimps, Monkeys & Lemurs
23 – Herbaceous Borders
24 – Walk-through Aviary
25 – Parking
26 – Flamingos
27 – Bird Pens
28 – Small Orchard
29 – Aviary
30 – Coypu (1937)
31 – Polar Bear (1932)
32 – Porcupines
33 – Fallow Deer

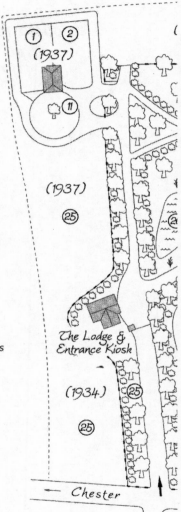

Riding School (purchase[d]

① ②
(1937)
⑪

(1937)
㉕

The Lodge &
Entrance Kiosk

(1934) ㉕

㉕

← Chester

Map drawn by George Williams

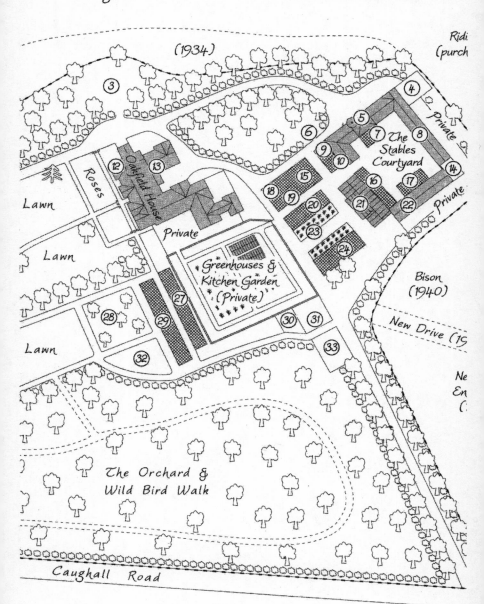

The Zoo boundary when it first opened in 1931

Additional land with year of purchase

0 5 10 15 20 25
yards

(1934)

Ridi
(purch

Private

Private

The Stables
Courtyard

Roses

Oakfield House

Private

Lawn

Lawn

Lawn

Greenhouses &
Kitchen Garden
(Private)

Bison
(1940)

New Drive (19

Ne
En
(

The Orchard &
Wild Bird Walk

Caughall Road

Introduction

One evening, late in 2010, I had a phone call from a young man called Adam Kemp. The name meant nothing to me, but at my age that's hardly surprising. He had been brought up in the Wirral, he said, and had regularly gone on outings to Chester Zoo when he was a boy, but hadn't been back since. Until that weekend that is, when he was up visiting his parents and had gone to the zoo, where he'd read a series of posters where the old aquarium used to be about the zoo's history: how it was started by my father and how we'd all lived there together – my grandparents as well as Dad and my mum and my sister Muriel and me – and how it all so nearly didn't happen.

'The thing is,' he said, 'I'm a TV producer, and I think the story of the zoo and your family would make a great drama series. So I wondered if I could come and see you and have a chat?'

My husband Fred, whom I'd been married to for sixty-three happy years said, 'Why not?'

'It won't be instantaneous, mind,' my

young visitor had warned as we said goodbye after that first meeting, during which we'd talked for what seemed like hours. 'It could be months before we hear anything. TV is like that I'm afraid.' He wasn't exaggerating: it would be over three years before shooting started.

My husband's casual 'Why not?' was so typical of him – always looking round the next corner, ready for the next adventure. A few weeks after Adam Kemp's visit, we went to spend Christmas in Indonesia with our eldest daughter, who was working as a teacher in Jakarta. During our stay we took a trip out to the Gili Islands off the coast of Lombok, where Fred and Joy went snorkelling together and, among other things, he found himself swimming alongside a hawksbill turtle – not bad for someone in their mid-eighties. We had always been great travellers – the kind who backpack rather than stay in luxury hotels or go on organised tours – and this wasn't our first visit to Southeast Asia by any means, but it would be our last. That June Fred was diagnosed with oesophageal cancer and was given six months to live.

I wanted to call the whole TV thing off, but he wouldn't hear of it. 'You never know,' he said. 'It could be fun.' The next few months were dreadful, and I'm not going to spell it out except to say that he faced it with his usual fortitude and good humour, our children were marvellous and we all spent a happy last Christmas together. He passed away in January 2012.

To everyone's surprise – particularly mine – the TV drama was still going ahead. And Fred, as so often, was right. It was fun, another adventure. Since shooting started, I have had some of the most exciting weeks of my life, finding myself part of a whole new family, getting to grips with a whole new world.

Of course the drama series was different from how things were in real life. It wasn't like time travel. For a start, it wasn't shot at Oakfield. Although the original house and outbuildings haven't changed that much, a film crew would have disrupted the daily life of the zoo. More importantly, you couldn't bring in animals from outside. As for Upton, when we moved there in 1931 it was just a dozen or so cottages stretched along the road, with a shop, a post office and a little school, all backed by fields. It bears no resemblance now to how it looked eighty years ago. So, for those scenes, they used a village about fifteen miles away. For the house, they found a large mansion near Warrington, red brick like Oakfield, covered it with fake ivy, and hey presto.

As for my character, someone asked

recently if I felt strange seeing myself being portrayed by a young actress. The answer is no. They needed 'June' to be older than four, which was my real age in 1931. Never for one moment did I imagine I was watching my alter ego (she was much prettier than I was for a start). Then there were the animals. For about six years my best friend was a chimpanzee called Mary, but you can't use chimps in films anymore, so no Mary.

'That's what I call taking liberties,' my friend Nancy said when I told her. 'What's wrong with the real story, why do they need to change it?' Nancy and I have been friends since school – her family had a farm the other side of Upton – and she was one of the few people I felt comfortable with bringing back home. I told her I didn't see it like that. 'It's not a documentary. It's a drama,' I said, repeating the phrase that had been used by the television people. And it's true; in real life your cast of characters is far too big. There are too many strands – most of which go nowhere – and things happen over too long a period of time. In real life my mother had three brothers then living – so I had three Atkinson uncles – whereas in the drama I had one. It's what's called 'poetic licence'. And that's fine by me. Because, in spite of all the differences, there were moments when I had goose bumps and a shiver ran down my spine and I thought, 'That's just how it was.'

Because the important story, that of my parents' struggle, was still there at the heart of it.

The credits say *Our Zoo* was inspired by the story of George Mottershead. And that's what my father was: inspirational. What he started in an empty Victorian mansion, which had in its time been a gentleman's residence and then a home for Belgian officers in the First World War, is now counted among the top zoos of the world. I know it. Other zoo directors know it. But now millions of ordinary people will know it too. And all I ever wanted was for my parents to have the recognition they deserved.

In another way, Nancy was right. The real story of the Mottershead family and Chester Zoo might not have involved as many romantic attachments (though mine and Fred's stands up there with the best), but it's just as dramatic and it too deserves the telling.

June Mottershead,
Upton-by-Chester, September 2014

Chapter 1

My earliest real memory is of the night we arrived at Oakfield in a removals van. It was 7 December 1930 and there was me, my mother, my sister, a woolly monkey, two goats and two lovebirds. I was four and my sister Muriel was fourteen. Father wasn't with us as he was in Derbyshire collecting bears, which he'd been offered at a knock-down price if he could trap them. They would be more or less the zoo's first animals.

We'd had great trouble in finding the little gate that led to the estate. The house hadn't been lived in for a while and the garden was quite overgrown – yew and holly and rhododendrons that had got out of hand – almost hidden by trees and hedges on both sides. The roads we'd come on were narrow country lanes – no houses and no signposts. It was pitch-dark and very cold, so we didn't see anything of the house but followed the drive up to the front door.

Muriel, the van driver and my mother unloaded the furniture and left it in the hall that was bigger than any of the rooms in our old house – and Mum lit candles so we could see. While Mum and Mew sorted out the animals, I waited in the hall with the love-birds. It was so cold I could see my breath, and the house was completely bare, just floorboards and tiles, no carpets or curtains, and it echoed. As we needed somewhere to sleep, my sister and my mother carried the frame of my parents' double bed upstairs – luckily there was a great wide staircase that climbed around three sides of a high inner hall – and once they reached the top, Mum opened the first door she came to and this would be her bedroom for the rest of her life.

While I sat huddled in a corner, too tired to help, Mum and Muriel went back downstairs and hauled up the big feather mattress, then back they went again for the other bedding and, last of all, the eiderdown, which they heaped on top.

We were so cold that first night that we didn't undress but all got in together, Mother, Muriel and Me. It's strange what you remember as a child. I needed to go to the lavatory, but as we didn't know the layout of the house, my mother went back downstairs for my potty. Not seeing where she was going, she bumped into one of the pillars on the way back up, and you could see this big lump on her forehead in the candle-light, and I felt that it was all my fault.

These days, if a politician admits to having his wife or children on the payroll, eyes roll, because everyone assumes it's because of tax. But while my father, George Mottershead, was without doubt the driving force behind what would become Chester Zoo, it could never have happened without the rest of the family.

My mother's father, Thomas Atkinson, a hill farmer in the Lake District, provided the private mortgage that enabled Dad to buy the Oakfield estate when the bank turned him down. My mum's childhood on the remote Westmorland Fells taught her all she needed to know about self-sufficiency and animal husbandry, while ten years in service – she didn't marry my father until she was twenty-seven – meant there was nothing she didn't know about feeding a large household.

On the Mottershead side, Dad's father Albert was a nurseryman in charge of everything to do with the zoo's gardens. By the time he was thirty he had been head gardener in a mansion in Didsbury called Brockhurst, responsible for several acres, full of specimen trees and flowers, a conservatory, cold frames and greenhouses – all the trappings of a well-to-do Victorian merchant who, thanks to the railway, could work in Manchester and lead the life of a country squire at the same time. Granddad's employer, a Mr William Brockbank, was an amateur horticulturist. These were the days when botanists were travelling the world in search of exotic plants and collecting was all the rage. As well as their cargo of cotton or sugar, ships arriving at the Liverpool docks would be carrying seeds and cuttings and saplings destined for greenhouses like Mr Brockbank's. This was when Granddad developed his passion for alpine primulas – auriculas – which he never lost, winning prizes in specialist flower shows across Britain, eventually becoming a judge.

As for my grandmother, Lucy, she had brought up seven children – only four of them her own, Granddad being a widower when they met. She too had been in service for many years – she was thirty-four when she and Granddad wed. She was his second wife and, although it was never even whispered, he probably remarried to provide a step-mother for the three children from his first marriage (his wife had died of cancer when she was only thirty-four). As it turned out, it was a real love match. Granddad was a gentle giant, well over six feet tall, while Granny's head barely reached his chest.

Finally there was my sister Muriel, ten years older than me. Mew, as we called her, had always loved animals and at the age of fourteen – just days after she left school – she became Oakfield's first keeper. As the zoo grew and we took on staff on the animal side, Mew was their overall boss, second only to Dad in the hierarchy.

Even my husband Fred would play his

part. He arrived after the war as a keeper, but ended up as clerk of works, helping to turn my father's dreams into reality. Fred and my dad were quite a pair, both of them capable of making something out of nothing, and in double-quick time. Laziness was something my dad could never understand or put up with.

As for me, when we moved to Oakfield in 1930, I was more of a nuisance than a help. But once my dad learnt the value of marketing, and how a photo of a little girl with an animal would melt a newspaper editor's heart like nothing else, I earned my keep. But perhaps it's only now that I have found my most valuable role, as chronicler of the struggles and successes of our family, the friends and foes, the depression, the war, and finally recognition and the knowledge that it wasn't in vain.

As anyone who knew him would have agreed, George Mottershead was a force to be reckoned with. What for others would have been a setback, my father saw as a challenge, and a challenge was just another word for opportunity. If he set his mind to something, he would do it, and if he couldn't do it himself, he'd persuade somebody else to do it for him. He could charm the birds off the trees, and most other animals too, come to that, including humans – particularly the ladies.

His life-changing moment came when he was eight years old. In June 1902, to celebrate the end of the Second Boer War, my granddad took George and his little brother Stanley to Belle Vue Zoo in Manchester. It started as a tearoom in 1836, with a small menagerie, decorative cages of monkeys and parrots. It was a little way out from the centre and you needed a carriage to get there, so it was really only for the gentry. But ten years on, with the coming of the railways and workers flooding into Manchester's cotton mills, the emphasis changed. By 1902 Belle Vue was advertising itself as 'the showground of the world'. As well as the animals, there was an amusement park, a dirt-racing track, various sports, a dance hall and even a circus. In the summer they had firework displays on an island in the boating lake.

It must have been quite an adventure for those two small boys – my father and my uncle – taking the train from where they lived south of the city, where my granddad was now working for the Sale Moor Nursery.

Sale, on the fertile land between the River Mersey and the River Dee, was originally just a collection of farms. But the opening of the Bridgewater Canal in the eighteenth century provided a cheap route for growers to take fruit and vegetables to Manchester. The coming of the railways made it even easier, and by the 1920s Sale was one big market garden.

Even at the age of eight, my dad knew about animals. He helped my granddad build an aviary, where they kept finches, cockatiels and budgerigars. He had his own collection of beetles and lizards – creatures that came in as stowaways among the plants that arrived at the Liverpool docks. And Granddad let him have a henhouse, where he kept Plymouth Rock hens that he'd reared from chicks. But the prospect of seeing real wild animals made him near sick with excitement. I heard him tell the story so many times, never quite the same admittedly, but never so different as to make you not believe it happened.

Instead of being thrilled, however, he was shocked. He'd seen pictures of elephants – prints probably, set in their natural habitat – but here was the reality: this noble creature, pressing its great head against thick iron bars with spikes on top, like a prison. From time to time it would uncoil its trunk and push it through the bars to catch a swinging rope, pulling on it to ring a bell. Then the watching crowd would throw it sweets and titbits as a reward, which it would catch and transfer to its soft pink mouth while the watchers whistled and jeered. It was the same for the other animals – the lions and monkeys, chimpanzees and giraffes.

Young as he was, George felt they were not treated with the respect they deserved. On the way home he was silent. Then, over supper that night, he announced that he knew what he wanted to do when he grew up to be a man. He was going to build a zoo, he said. A zoo without bars.

Five years later my father left school. In those days, unless you were exceptional and could get a scholarship to somewhere like Manchester Grammar, there was nothing for it but to get a job. While still helping Albert in the nursery, he set himself up as a physical culture instructor, what we would now call body-building. Pictures of that time – he posed for a camera club in a series of classical 'attitudes' – show that he had a good physique. Where he got the idea from I can't imagine, but it would serve him well.

In the summer of 1914 Britain found itself at war with Germany. At first there was no conscription, and although records have been lost, it seems likely that George didn't enlist straight away. For one thing, he wouldn't have wanted to lose his physical culture patrons – built up over a number of years by then – for a war that everyone said would be 'over by Christmas'. However, his brother Stanley was among the first wave of volunteers. Four years younger than George, it must have seemed like a great adventure.

He was a 'Manchester Pal', joining the 19th Battalion Manchester Regiment to do basic training in Heaton Park, the largest municipal park in Manchester until it became one of the largest military training grounds in the country. Then, after more training in Lincolnshire and on Salisbury Plain, Stanley embarked for France in September 1915.

George joined the South Lancashires sometime that autumn. At Christmas he was home on leave, and on 19 January he married my mum – Elizabeth Atkinson, Lizzie as he called her. I have no idea how they met or how long they'd known each other, but I doubt if they were childhood sweethearts, because he was only twenty-one while she was twenty-seven, but she'd been in service in Sale just a few streets away from where the Mottersheads lived. Dad must have still been stationed locally – possibly in Heaton Park, looking after the horses – because in March my sister Muriel was conceived. By April he too had left for the front.

His battalion took part in the Battle of the Somme, and on 15 October 1916 he was severely injured when a bullet went through the left side of his neck, grazing his spine as it went. He ended up at Highfield Military Hospital in Knotty Ash, Liverpool, when the family were told that he would end his days in a wheelchair.

He was still in hospital on 7 December

1916 when Muriel was born. When my mother went in to show him his new daughter, the other wounded soldiers held a sweepstake to choose her name. Whether it was one of my dad's money-making exercises I don't know, but I wouldn't put it past him.

It was a terrible time for my grandparents. George was paralysed for life and shortly after Christmas came the news that Stanley had been killed, three days before Muriel was born. He was eighteen. Nine months after that, they learnt that Albert, my grandfather's second son from his first marriage, had also fallen in action.

Nor was that the end. Two of my mother's brothers, James and Thomas, had been in France since the beginning of the war. James was killed in January 1917, aged only twenty-two, and Thomas went missing in April 1918, aged twenty-seven, just seven months before the Armistice. In some ways this was the worst, as Thomas's body was never found. For years afterwards my grandmother, Hannah, would start at any knock on the door of their farm, thinking that it might be him, that he'd maybe lost his memory or been taken as a prisoner of war, unable to come home.

What it must have been like to live with all that I can't imagine. But it goes some way to explaining Dad's stubbornness; his refusal to give in, whatever was stacked against him; the responsibility he bore to make something of his life.

Dad was now the eldest remaining son of his parents' marriage. Albert wasn't getting any younger, and Lucy wasn't far behind, and who was going to look after them in their old age if he didn't? Although the old-age pension had recently been introduced, it wasn't much – 7/6d a week for a married couple in 1911, and the qualifying age was seventy. Albert had turned sixty in 1916. In fact he would live until he was ninety-three. There was also Charlie, born in 1900, Dad's youngest brother, who had been too young to go to war. Plus he now had a wife and baby to think of. In hospital they had written him off – his physiotherapy had consisted mainly of needlework, and he sewed his own buttons on his shirts all his life.

Somehow my dad's knowledge of muscles, his level of fitness, his discipline, as well as his sheer determination, began to take effect. First he found he could move his arms. Then, using crutches, he forced his legs to respond. Bearing his weight on his shoulders, he would negotiate the stairs down from their flat to the street then slowly make his way to Granddad's nursery, where he'd walk up and down the beaten earth between the rows of vegetables and flowers, forwards and backwards, backwards and forwards. It wasn't like a story from the Bible – he didn't throw his crutches on the compost heap and start running – but within three years he could walk unaided. It was only when he got into his seventies that his limp returned, otherwise you'd never have known he'd been injured, let alone so badly, though he never smoked, at a time when everybody did. That bullet had done for his lungs, he said.

For a few years George was still little use to Albert in the nursery. But he didn't waste his time. He went to night school and took classes in accountancy and carpentry and made ends meet by breeding and selling birds. Pets such as dogs were expensive to feed, but birds were cheap to look after. In the days before the radio, a canary or some other kind of songbird – or a budgerigar from Australia that could entertain you with its mimicry – was within the reach of ordinary folk. Not only did they bring a splash of colour into people's lives, they were company.

Once the army learned that George Mottershead had got back the use of his legs, they stopped his disability pension. Medical advice was that he should 'live an open-air life', and by borrowing from his father-in-law, he bought a smallholding thirty miles south of Sale, between the villages of Hough and Shavington, just outside Crewe. The new little family – Mum, Dad and Muriel, as well as Granddad and Granny – moved there early in 1919.

34

Crewe, as anyone of a certain generation will know, lies on the main line from London to the north. It was the headquarters of the Grand Junction Railway, and the biggest junction in the country, with connections to Wales, Chester, Liverpool and Birmingham. Crewe itself, which had been a farming community before the railway arrived, was now a sizeable town, sprawling over acres of sidings and locomotive sheds where engines were built and maintained.

The smallholding in Shavington was called Oakfield – one of those coincidences that are hard to explain, though oak trees are very common in the area. It ran to seven and a half acres, including greenhouses, soft-fruit cages and sheds. At first things continued much as they had done in Sale, with Granddad growing produce which Dad would take to Crewe every morning in a pony and trap and put on the Manchester train. But within a year, my father had taken a shop in Mill Street, where Granddad's produce could be sold direct to the public.

As well as flowers and vegetables, Granddad grew soft fruit like strawberries, raspberries, gooseberries and blackcurrants, and there were apples, pears and plums from the orchard. They had a cow called Molly who they got for her milk, and there were pigs. The pigs lived on windfalls and slops from the kitchen, as well as vegetables that weren't good enough to go to the shop. My mother kept hens and sold eggs and dressed chickens.

Muriel, who was only four when the family arrived at Shavington, would tell me stories about those early days, remembering how hard they had all worked. Mum would be cleaning and dressing the birds in the back kitchen late into the night, to be ready for the Christmas rush. She also made up bouquets from Granddad's flowers, and at Christmas there would be holly wreaths, and Mum and Dad would go off on their bikes to collect moss, coming home cold and wet. Muriel remembered how she'd be sitting with Granddad by the fire, waiting for them to get back, surrounded by great piles of holly and him wiring it all up.

They worked long hours, starting at first light. Granny's job was to keep the house, do the cooking and look after Muriel, who stayed at home until she was seven, when she started at the Ursuline convent in Crewe – paid for by my other grandfather. No one in the family was Catholic – in fact, apart from Granny, they weren't religious at all – it was just that my mother considered Muriel would get a better education with the nuns.

Although Granny stopped going to church when we moved to Upton – the vicar was one of the main objectors to the zoo – she was always quite 'proper'. She made sure our fingernails were clean and that we brushed our hair a hundred times before going to bed. She was definitely not modern. She wore skirts that reached nearly down to the ground and never cut her hair, but wore it coiled up on her head in a bun. It had been her crowning glory when she was young, she told me, the colour of chestnuts, but by the time I knew her it was white. She had grown up in a town – her father had been a tailor in Doncaster in Yorkshire – and she taught us to sew and to darn. She never really felt comfortable in the country and was happiest if she didn't have to go outside. Muriel remembered how much she had hated the pigs. To her, they were 'them dirty things' and she'd chase them out of the freshly sluiced yard with a bucket. In fact she didn't really like animals at all and this was the case right through her life.

Mum was totally the opposite. She was born on her parents' farm on a remote fellside in Westmorland, one of eight children – the name, Hunger Hill Farm, says it all. Even their nearest neighbours were a good distance away, and in winter it was hard to walk the two miles to the nearest school and Sunday school, as likely as not through biting wind. She would tell me about the orphan lambs that she would be given to rear, her dad finding them buried in drifts and bringing them into the kitchen, nearly given up for dead, and Mum warming them back to life in her lap and feeding them drop by drop until they were strong enough to take a bottle. This was always my favourite bedtime story; I could hear it again and again – the names of the lambs, how they would follow her around just as if she was their mother.

To her, animals were her family; she treated them all as individuals, each one had its own name and character. Every evening she would do the rounds, checking they had water and clean straw and were settled for the night. To do this at Shavington wasn't difficult, because there weren't that many, but it was the same at Upton. She would no more have gone to bed without saying goodnight to each and every one of them than not look in on me and give me a kiss.

By now Dad had started buying things in for the shop – fancy pots and vases, and bulbs and bulb bowls from Holland. Mum was now pregnant, and in 1924 my brother Frankie was born. Having a son was important in those days because it meant there'd be someone to carry on the family business, whereas a daughter would marry and leave home. Sadly Frankie caught whooping cough and died eleven months later. There was a doctor in the village – Dr Winkle – but there was nothing he could do. There were no antibiotics till after the Second World War and children died all the time. Granddad had lost two daughters: Eva in infancy at three weeks and Nora aged fourteen with TB.

It might have been commonplace, but that didn't make losing Frankie any easier and my mother kept a framed photo of him above her bed all her life. It had been taken at a studio in Crewe when he was about six months old. He was dressed in white, and had blond hair, pale eyes and a sweet, open-looking face. He'd been photographed sitting on Muriel's lap, but when Mum had it enlarged after he died, Mew was cut out. I used to lie on her bed and look up at it and think about what he would have been like – the brother I never knew.

Meanwhile the business had expanded, with Dad taking over the shop next door, which previously had been a milliner's. After selling off the existing stock, he filled it with exotic birds and small animals. Except for parrots, he bred the birds himself, but he also sold fish, reptiles, white mice and guinea pigs, as well as the hutches and cages and feeders to go with them. There were tortoises that arrived in big round tins holding dozens of them, all piled on top of each other. These had to be washed and cleared of ticks, and finally the shells were polished with oil. He even had a monkey or two as an attraction, to get people interested enough to go into the shop.

Although there'd been something of a boom in the years immediately after the war – the roaring twenties – by 1924 mining was in trouble. Heavy use of coal during the war resulted in rich seams being mined out. Also overseas markets had been lost: Germany was providing free coal to France and Italy as part of the war reparations. The mine owners' answer was to reduce miners' pay. The unions responded with the slogan, 'Not a penny off pay, not a second on the day'. To avoid an all-out clash, the Conservative government stepped in and said they would provide subsidies to keep colliers' pay at its current level, but only for nine months – so all this did was give the owners time to prepare.

The result was the General Strike that lasted ten days from 3–13 May 1926, when the whole country came to a standstill. But in the end it failed. A million miners were locked out and never re-employed. It was the same with the railway unions, who'd supported the miners since the beginning. For somewhere like Crewe, it was devastating, and for Dad's shop, it spelled ruin. Former railway workers who had allotments could grow their own vegetables, and no one could think of buying flowers or keeping pets. The shop quickly went bust. Luckily Shavington was in my mother's name, but everything else with a value had to go: the cow, the hens and the pigs. Mum was heartbroken and wept for days. But no one wanted exotic birds or inedible fish, however pretty they were. Worse, people were soon returning animals they'd bought from the shop because they couldn't afford to feed them, and Dad would never turn an animal away.

Granddad went back to growing produce for Manchester market. But his flower borders still looked beautiful, and eventually someone said, 'What about opening a little zoo and charging folks to come in?' So that's what happened. The tomato house was used for birds and small animals, while the henhouse became a monkey house. Paths were cut, borders enlarged, benches were put out so visitors could sit and enjoy it all. What had been a summer house became a café and shop selling postcards and sweets, and Mum was run off her feet because by then she also had a three-year-old to look after. I had been born on 21 June 1926, just a month after the end of the General Strike, when the bailiffs were already banging at the door.

Chapter 2

It shouldn't have worked, but it did. People began coming in droves, not from Crewe, where things were still terrible, but from the other direction, the Potteries – Stoke-on-Trent, Burslem and Hanley in north Staffordshire, which was only fifteen miles away and had been barely affected by the strike. Crosville, the local bus company, set up a regular service to ferry visitors who came by train, from the north and even from Wales. They also came in cars and in charabancs, hundreds every week. Entry was 6d, with children under twelve half price. At the bottom of the advertising leaflet was written: 'The finest collection of Rare Animals and Birds in the Provinces.' This was a quote from an article in an illustrated magazine called *Town and Country News*, which I still have. It also said, 'Mr Mottershead is to be congratulated upon his work of national importance, a work which speaks volumes for his zoological knowledge and his organising abilities.' The main attraction, it said, was the monkey house, where Babs the chimp was the star turn.

Refreshments are brought to her each afternoon by the only waitress whom she will permit to serve her. If they are late, or the waitress is tardy in her movements, 'Babs' shows her impatience by a continuous knocking on the table. The refreshments usually consist of cocoa and cake, and as an indication of her superiority, socially and otherwise, over the rest of the monkey house, she holds her cup quite correctly and generally adopts perfect table manners.

The waitress of course was Muriel. Also in the monkey house, the reporter continued, were:

Humboldt's Woolly or spider Monkeys with young, Tite Monkeys, Mona Monkey with young, Douroucouli monkey, Sooty and Grivet Monkeys, Golden Arm Squirrel Monkey, Common or white Shouldered Marmosets, Black Tamarins and a pair of Gorgeous Lion Marmosets.

Just outside the Monkey House are a magnificent pair of Giant African Porcupines and a little further on, in quite a unique enclosure, are two Canadian Black Bears, adjoining them is a rabbit warren where rabbits of all colours live in a natural setting.

Birds, he wrote, were one of the glories of the gardens and the collection was as beautiful as it was rare. The lorikeets included

43

porphyry-crowned, green-naped, Forsten's and blue mountain.

As I was only three when this was written, I can remember very few of the animals he talks about, except for Babs, the bears and the rabbits. My favourites among the birds were a pair of hyacinth macaws, which don't even get a mention. They are brilliant-blue parrots from Brazil and were as long as I was tall. There was also an African grey who talked like a navvy, Granny said. I do remember the African porcupines because Muriel reared them from babies.

I remember the woolly monkey and the lion marmosets, which I liked, but there were also some macaque monkeys, which I hated because they were noisy and given half the chance would pull your hair or bite your ear. My favourite was a ring-tailed lemur called Lulu, whose striped tail stood up at right angles and who I would wear round my shoulders like a shawl because her grey fur was as soft as silk. Her hands were so delicate – with their tiny fingers and tiny nails – I could spend hours playing with them.

And the animals kept coming. Even before the zoo, Dad had boarding kennels for dogs – my favourite was a white Pekinese. He hated leaving animals in the small cages they arrived in. They needed fresh air and room to fly or to swing, he said, and he would work as quickly as he could to get their new quarters built. There was no shortage of space – the shortage was money, as even the most basic pens needed wire mesh, and that didn't grow on trees. Labour, however, was never a problem. Ever since the war there had been men tramping the roads looking for work, sleeping rough and living off whatever they could get. People were generally kind and helped when they were able because there wasn't a family in the country that hadn't lost a son or a brother. The road to Crewe went right past our door and my mum never turned them away. She couldn't give money or even a day's paid employment, but they never went away with an empty stomach. They were always so grateful, she said, it made her want to weep. And if they could help, they would.

In January 1930 the number of visitors to the zoo was 800. The café had now been enlarged and had proper glass windows and a paraffin heater. Money – or the lack of it – was the only thing holding him back, Dad said, so he went into partnership with a Dr William English, who practised in Crewe and whom he'd known since opening the shop. They had a shared interest in animals, and Dr English was a member of the Royal Zoological Society.

With Muriel at school all day, I would spend most of my time with the animals. I would sit with the bears and talk to them for hours about what I was doing, about how naughty the macaques were and how Muriel would soon be back from the convent. They didn't talk back, or take much notice of me at all, but then it was often the same with grown-ups. It didn't mean they didn't understand.

With Babs, it was different. I would make patterns in the ground with a stick and she would copy, making marks in the sawdust on her side of the cage. I can still remember her hands picking at my clothes through the wire – they were wrinkled like an old man's though she was only a baby. When Muriel came back from school she would open Babs's cage to let me play with her. She was able to write letters with a pencil on paper – Muriel had taught her how – whereas I could only scratch shapes in the dirt.

It wasn't long before my dad and his partner fell out. Dr English was trying to tell him how to run things and even brought in another director without Dad's say-so. The final straw was something to do with the marmosets and how they should be housed. Once they realised it wasn't going to work, they argued about who should buy whom out. First Dr English said he would go. But in the end it was Dad who left. He had ambition, he said. Dr English had none.

Under the terms of their agreement, Dr

English would keep the animals and continue to run the zoo in the way he wanted, so at the end of July we moved to lodgings in Mill Street in Crewe, next to Mum and Dad's friends, the Buckleys, who ran a baby-linen shop, while Dad decided what to do next. In fact he already knew. He was going to open another zoo, like Shavington only bigger. All he needed was the right premises.

The summer of 1930 wasn't the most auspicious time to start any new business venture, let alone something as unconventional as a zoo, but Dad said it was 'now or never'. Wall Street had crashed a little over six months before and the London Stock Exchange hadn't been far behind. The effect was worst in the north of the country, as heavy industry ground to a halt and affected everything else. One consequence was that large country estates were going cheap. In the nineteenth century industrialists and mill owners had built lavish houses for themselves that needed armies of staff to run. What with the war, and then the crash, prices had plummeted because nobody had a use for them anymore. Except my dad.

He concentrated his search for a property with grounds suitable for a zoo in Cheshire and Derbyshire. Then, six weeks after he began looking with a friend called Mr Eaton who had a car, he saw the Oakfield estate in

47

the village of Upton-by-Chester, twenty-four miles north-west of Crewe and knew immediately that he'd found what he was looking for. Oakfield was a handsome red-brick mansion, set in nine acres, and included two orchards and a walled kitchen garden with glasshouses and cucumber and melon frames. There was a large stable block enclosing a cobbled courtyard, a conservatory in a good state of repair, one part of which was a hothouse, one part vinery, and a pond in the central section. Although the garden hadn't been tended for over a year, you could still see the bones of the landscaping. There was a rose garden and a separate lodge. Best of all, it was only two miles from the centre of Chester, in an area earmarked for development. Planning for a major bypass had recently been approved in order to provide a fast road to Birkenhead and Liverpool. There was also railway access at Upton-by-Chester Halt, with regular trains to both Chester and Birkenhead less than a mile away.

The estate dated from the mid-nineteenth century, but in 1895 the original house had been extensively remodelled by a wealthy tea merchant, Benjamin Chaffers Roberts, Lord Mayor of Chester and later High Sheriff of Cheshire. During the First World War it had been a convalescent home for stranded Belgian officers, who had been billeted in temporary huts in the grounds. It was now owned by a cotton millionaire who'd gone bust as a result of the crash and was desperate to sell.

When the estate agent asked him how many bedrooms he required, my father replied, 'Three or ten, it doesn't matter.' What was important, he said, was that it was screened from the road. He was so secretive, the agent concluded he was planning to set up a nudist colony, but he just believed animals needed peace and quiet, far away from the noise of traffic on a busy road.

Now all my father had to do was agree a price. He already knew something about running a business. He knew about bookkeeping from his accountancy classes, and he also had practical experience. The shop in Crewe had made money until the General Strike. The zoo at Shavington had also made money. He had done his sums and he was convinced this would work. The only stumbling block was raising the capital...

On 19 August he began negotiations. On 18 September he took out an option to buy Oakfield at £3,500. For what it was, this was a knock-down price – the equivalent now of about £250,000 – when, eighteen months earlier, it would have been six times as much, if not more.

Apart from two fields he still owned at Shavington, he had no collateral to offer as security and the bank would only lend him £2,300 for six months. Once again his father-in-law, my Westmorland grandfather, came to the rescue with a private mortgage. The Atkinsons had lost two sons in the war and Mum's sister had died of diabetes aged only twenty-six. Perhaps this was why they wanted to help their only remaining daughter, but they weren't doing it for nothing. My grandfather wasn't rich – he was only a tenant farmer on the Lowther estate, the land leased from the Earl of Lonsdale – and he demanded the same rate of interest Dad would have paid a bank. On 18 October George Mottershead put down a non-returnable deposit of £350. His plan was to raise money locally through well-to-do residents in the area who would be interested in investing in such an enterprising venture which was of benefit to the local community. On 23 October, the conveyance well underway, his solicitors put in an application to the Chester Rural District Council for use of the Oakfield estate as a zoological gardens and café. As there were no restrictions on the sale, Dad was told this was only a formality.

The plan was to open in time for the Easter and Whitsun bank holidays, the most important days in any zoo's calendar. (Just under 90,000 people had visited London Zoo over Easter in 1928, breaking all records.) Easter that year, 1931, fell on 5 April, only four months away, and Granny and Granddad moved into the lodge the moment they could. My grandparents were as involved in the new venture as Mum and Dad were. While Dad would oversee everything to do with the animals, the garden and the growing of all the vegetables was down to Granddad. Although the planting of the formal gardens had largely survived, there was still a lot to do. The drive and paths were buried under drifts of leaves a foot deep, all of which had to be cleared. It was practically a botanical garden, Granddad said, and he was already compiling an inventory of what plants were there, listing what could be split, what propagated and what needed to be bought in. Seeds needed sowing in the glasshouses for summer bedding and the ground prepared for early vegetable crops. The vinery needed fumigating and the grape vine pruned. In the central section of the conservatory geraniums had to be trained up the wall and tiered stages made for the display of orchids and other frost-tender plants. This would double as the reptile house and they would need plenty of cover. Elsewhere, undergrowth had to be cleared, azaleas and rhododendrons thinned and mulched, hedges trimmed, perennials split, manure spread and the vegetable garden double-dug. It was a task that would have taxed someone half his age, and Granddad was now seventy-four.

In the meantime word had got round that George Mottershead, formerly of Shavington Zoological Gardens, was looking for animals, and he'd been contacted by the Matlock Bath Corporation. Matlock Bath was a spa resort just south of Matlock in the Peak District, over two hours' drive away. A narrow ravine had been turned into a spa after hot springs had been discovered a hundred years earlier. An additional visitor attraction was a small menagerie that included two Canadian black bears housed in a cave in the side of the cliff that ran alongside the river. Although spacious enough, headroom was limited and the bears could no longer stand up, so they had to go. Adam and Eve were Dad's for £28, the manager said, a bargain considering they'd cost the corporation £50 only nine months earlier.

Dad and Mr Buckley – Dad couldn't drive – set off for Matlock Bath one morning in early December. They had hired a Pantechnicon, the largest van available in those days, with a back door hinged at floor level that doubled as a ramp.

Matlock Bath wasn't known as Little Switzerland for nothing. Access to the cave was via a narrow footbridge over the ravine and their first job was to haul one of the crates across. They soon had an audience. Once in place, the gate across the cave mouth was unbolted and two keepers went in, intending to flush the bears out. Suddenly a howl went up and the onlookers watched as the two keepers made a hasty escape. They admitted they'd never set foot in there before and Eve had decided to go for them. Then it was Dad's turn, tempting them with apples. They quickly polished them off, but made no move. Next he tried honey. Still nothing.

Eventually, after about three hours of coaxing, Adam and Eve retired for the night, disappearing into the depths of their cave to their sleeping quarters. Dad and Mr Buckley slept in the van.

The next morning they tried again, and this time the apples-and-honey trick worked. Eve followed the trail and she was soon safely in the crate. But Adam was not so easily bought. As the hours ticked by, Eve became increasingly restless and the crate began to creak alarmingly. So Dad found a blacksmith, who secured it with additional iron bands. The next morning was spent reinforcing the crate and lining it with sheet metal.

The third attempt found Adam pacing up and down. He was clearly in a very bad temper. The only option, Dad now decided, was to sedate him, so they got hold of a vet. Not surprisingly, this country vet's experience of bears was limited, and he had no idea what dose it would take to make him docile. First he tried an apple studded with chloral hydrate. Adam wolfed it down and everyone waited for him to get drowsy. Nothing happened. Next they tried chloroform. Adam sniffed the rags that had been soaked with it, but just continued to prowl up and down. The last attempt was to up the chloral hydrate dose, this time with the drug hidden in honey, which he devoured, but seemingly to no ill effect.

As it grew dark, the crowd that had gathered to watch the fun began to disperse. The first day's efforts had been covered by local newspapers and then picked up by the nationals, such as the *News Chronicle*, under the headline: EVE FALLS FOR THE APPLE BUT ADAM WON'T BITE. But now even the reporters had left. Refusing to accept defeat, Dad decided he would just have to go in there himself and Mr Buckley agreed to go with him.

Arming themselves with broom handles, they opened the gate and slipped in. Once over the threshold, away from the floodlights which had been set up outside, it was pitch-black and they couldn't even see each other, but then the bear couldn't see them either, though, sensing their presence, he snarled and tried to stand erect, but the roof was so low that he hit his head and stumbled back on all fours again. No one had been inside for nine months and the place stank. Slowly

Dad and Mr Buckley edged their way around the dripping walls until they were at the rear of the cave and Adam, standing at the entrance, was clearly silhouetted in the floodlights. Suddenly he heard them and turned, reared up on his hind legs, hit his head on the roof again and staggered. Seizing their chance, Dad and Mr Buckley rushed at him, wielding their sticks and yelling, and Adam backed into the crate. In a matter of seconds Dad had shot the bolt home.

By now it was midnight. Having roused some workmen to help haul the crate across the footbridge to the van, where Eve was already asleep, they were finally on their way. They drove straight to Oakfield, arriving in the middle of the night, and – by now quite amenable – the two bears were moved into an old horsebox which, like the crate, had been lined with metal and which stood in the courtyard of the stable block.

The following morning I woke up late and didn't know where I was. Mum's eiderdown was familiar, and the brass knobs on the bed ... I was still dressed in yesterday's clothes. I got up and walked to the window. Looking out towards a huge cedar tree, I saw Muriel crossing the lawn, sparkling with frost, so I knocked on the windowpane and waved. Gradually it came back to me: arriving in the dark, lighting the candles, sitting in the hall with the lovebirds, coming upstairs. I'd needed to go to the lavatory in the middle of the night and Mum had gone down to the hall to fetch my potty. And there it still was. But where was Mum? I put on my shoes and tentatively made my way down the huge staircase, calling her name. Then Muriel ran in, her footsteps echoing around the big, empty house.

'Come and see our new bears,' she said. 'They're called Adam and Eve. But let's get your coat on first because otherwise you'll catch your death. It's freezing out there.' Holding my hand, she led me away from the hall, down a passage painted dark-green and out into the cold. Then along an icy path, and another, until we were standing in front of a gateway with a turret to one side, like one where a princess might let down her hair for a prince to climb up.

'In here,' she said, and we passed through a pretty iron gate under a high archway into a courtyard which was entirely enclosed by red-brick buildings, one-storey high, except where we'd come in. I ran to my mum and held on to her coat. She was talking to Dad and I knew better than to interrupt.

'So what do you think of your new home, June?' he eventually said.

'I thought we were going to live in a zoo.'

'We are.'

'So where are the animals?'

'They're going to be in here,' he said, turning around, demonstrating expansively with his hands. 'There'll be chimps over there, and monkeys in a big, high cage up against that wall, with plenty of room to climb and swing. And we'll have the aviary the other side. And in there, in the loose boxes where there used to be horses, there'll be different animals – ones you've never seen before! Ones you've never even heard of!'

For the next few days I went round in a trance. Could this magical place really be my new home? The house was beautiful. I fell in love with it then, and I still love it now, and sometimes wander through it in my dreams. There were chimney pots as tall as lamp posts, towering above the rooftops. The windows were as big as ones I'd seen in church, when I'd gone once with Granny, with patchworks of colour, and where the sun shone through it looked like rainbows. Downstairs – in the huge room where the café would be – there were friezes above the picture rail of animals and birds. The room Dad called the library – though there were no books – was panelled in dark, polished wood. And over the mantel, the wood was carved and rose nearly up to the ceiling.

Inset at each side of the fire grates were beautiful glazed tiles, different patterns and colours for every room – green and pink, yellow and red, decorated with flowers and birds. My favourite was in what had been the housekeeper's room in the servants' quarters, which we used as our family sitting room, and these were painted with robins.

We'd had an indoor lavatory at our other house, but here the bathrooms were the size of bedrooms – and not just one, but three! There was a bath with a brass canopy over the top, which was a shower. And another shower that had jets coming at you from the side, though it would be a long time until we had enough money to heat the water and try it out. Apart from the beds we'd brought with us, there wasn't a stick of furniture, no curtains, no carpets, no pictures. Just a few pots and pans that had disappeared straight into the kitchen, and that was it. Voices, footsteps, doors banging, everything echoed. And it was bitterly cold...

Although I wanted to help – and was always asking – there was nothing very much for me to do except to wander around and try to stay out of trouble. At Shavington I'd talked to the animals, but here there were only the new bears – whom I didn't know but who looked exactly like the bears we'd had at Shavington – the lovebirds, the woolly monkey and the goats, who spent their time wandering around the orchard, eating the grass and any rotten fruit they managed to find. I missed my old friends, especially

Babs, who I'd hoped would be waiting for me, but she had stayed in Shavington with Dr English, along with the old bears, Lulu the lemur and our parrots.

There was one game I discovered during those first few weeks that I never got tired of. In the servants' passage leading to the housekeeper's room there was a cupboard of noisy bells, each labelled with the name of one of the big rooms and connected to a bell push. In the old days these had been used to summon the servants. My game was to push the bell in the room, then race as fast as I could to get to the passage before the jangling stopped.

There had been bad news awaiting Dad when he got back from Matlock. On 27 November the planning application had been turned down. My father had known nothing about this meeting; neither had his solicitor. His letter in support of the application had not even been read, whereas several of the councillors had spoken against the proposal, saying things that were both unfounded and untrue. As he'd not been there, he'd been unable to refute the accusations. However, Dad's solicitor was optimistic that he could have the verdict overturned. The correct procedure had not been followed, he said. They should have been informed of the meeting and Dad had the right to be there – and that was sufficient reason to give them grounds for appeal. But all this took time.

Until Dad learnt to drive, he had to go everywhere by public transport, unless it was local, when he would bicycle. After driving back to Crewe with Mr Buckley to return the Pantechnicon, he had taken the bus to Nantwich to see his solicitor and then the bus back to Oakfield again, so everything took a very long time.

Upton-by-Chester had originally been a typical Cheshire village, a mixture of farmhouses and terraced cottages on Smoke Street and Sheep's Head Row, where cowherds and milkmaids would have lived in times gone by. It was still surrounded by dairy farms. Every morning we'd walk up to Cheers' Farm on the Caughall Road – which was the nearest to us – to fetch the milk, the empty quart churns clanking on their handles before the heavier journey home.

When the railway had arrived in 1839 – providing direct access to Chester and Birkenhead – substantial houses (of which Oakfield was the grandest) had begun to spring up, the kind of places that had gardeners and maids and butlers and cooks who, if not resident, lived in the terraced cottages in Sheep's Head Row. One of the large houses – the Lawns – belonged to Sir John Frost, who owned the Upton flour mill. He had been mayor of Chester between 1913 and 1919 and had influential friends. A few years earlier he had instigated the building of Upton village hall, holding a fundraising event in his garden that brought in nearly £2,000. The hall had had its grand opening in 1928, the ribbon being cut by Lady Arthur Grosvenor, sister-in-law of the Duke of Westminster, who had set up Oakfield for the use of Belgian officers during the war. The Rev. Toogood, vicar of Upton, was also from that world and he lived in some style in the rectory.

It was into this world of privilege that my father had unwittingly stumbled. The day after we moved into Oakfield, Dad took me with him into the village. He wanted to buy a newspaper, he said. There had been so many reporters standing around when he was picking up Adam and Eve, there was a good chance they'd written about it, which would be good publicity.

'Sorry to hear about your trouble,' a farm worker said as we came out of the shop.

'That's very kind of you,' Dad said. 'But I'm glad to say both bears are now back, safe and sound and doing well.'

The man looked puzzled. 'I was talking about the petition,' he said.

'Petition?'

'To stop you opening the zoo.' Although this man personally looked forward to having a zoo on his doorstep, he said, other Upton residents were up in arms and determined to stop it.

Although I was still only four, I can remember the cloud that hung over us for the next few months, the feeling of anxiety and apprehension that was always present. I saw it in my mum's face. I heard it in my grandmother's voice. Even Muriel would snap at me, which she never usually did. Dad had taken out this huge mortgage to buy Oakfield and interest had to be paid every month. He had been counting on the first paying visitors coming in at Easter. What was he to do? Throw more good money after bad in getting in more animals, making new enclosures, setting up the café? His hopes of raising money from the local well-to-do now looked unlikely. With no other options, he tried to raise another mortgage. But when he went to the bank he discovered that Sir John Frost, responsible for starting the petition, was a director...

In the meantime everyone worked. Even me. My mother cut holes in a potato sack for my head and arms and I helped paint the wire of the bears' enclosure. The café began to take shape. But the money leaked away. We had to have cups and saucers and plates. Teaspoons and teapots. New animals were arriving every day and needed to be fed. There were lots of new monkeys and a pair of coatis – a kind of South American racoon –

one red and one brown. There were also four new lemurs, though none of them as friendly as Lulu had been. There were two peacocks – or rather a peacock and a peahen – who immediately took up residence in the cedar tree. And the small orchard nearer the house, which was enclosed, had golden and silver and Lady Amherst pheasants from Burma. Later we had ordinary pheasants, as well as guinea fowl, who were allowed to roam around the gardens. I remember searching the shrubberies for their eggs, but usually all I would find was broken shells, the only evidence that they'd even laid, as they'd been eaten by foxes.

In the evenings, when I'd go out with Mum when she did her rounds, there'd be flashes of white as rabbits scattered at the sound of our voices. And most nights we'd catch glimpses of the foxes – long, dark shapes moving across the lawns like shadows. Birds were now busy building their nests and from early in the morning until well after dusk the garden was alive with their songs. Mum had been brought up in the country and she could pinpoint exactly who each song belonged to. We would look for the tawny owl, sitting high in the branches of the Scots pine outside the house. She'd show me the nests she'd found in the yew hedges and teach me how to tell the difference between a blackbird's and a song thrush's. Both lay pale-blue eggs, but a blackbird's has tiny black spots, while a thrush's has blurred red splodges. We'd look out for tiny goldcrests – smaller than a wren – on the cedar tree. We'd watch the hares playing in the moonlight in the fields beyond the garden and we'd leave a saucer of milk out by the back door for the visiting hedgehog. My mum gave me a love of nature that I've never lost.

Meanwhile rumours about Oakfield began to reach us, some of which found their way into the local press. It would be like Belle Vue Zoo in Manchester. There would be amusements, hurdy-gurdies, electric hare racing and a drag-car track. Dad himself was 'one of those menagerie people'. He would be breeding and training animals for circuses. There would be dirt and flies, as well as noise. With lions and tigers roaming around, local residents wouldn't be safe in their beds. Just as bad, it would bring the wrong class of visitor to Upton, who would end up by going to the pub and getting drunk. In the end there were 173 signatures on the petition. Meanwhile dad's solicitor had appealed the decision and the Ministry of Health was to conduct an enquiry. The date set was 6 February.

Dad knew that he had to play them at their own game and instructed a barrister to represent him at the hearing, to be held in Chester Town Hall. The barrister, Hugh Gamon, took Dad through his evidence. He was introduced as a fellow of the Royal Zoological Society – which he was by then, having followed Dr English's example. He explained that he had already run a successful small zoological garden in Shavington, also a residential area. His purpose in coming to Upton had been to find larger premises in which to keep a selection of small animals such as monkeys and porcupines, as well as foreign and English birds in an aviary. There would be a café for the convenience of visitors, but no 'attractions'. The emphasis would be on education. It was surely far better for children to see live animals than stuffed ones in a museum? And there were no lions and tigers, he said. There were only two pet bears who were as tame as Alsatians.

Asked by the solicitor representing the residents of Upton how he intended to finance the project, Dad said he expected about a hundred visitors a day, and there would also be season-ticket holders and income from the café to boost takings at the gate. 'So you intend to draw large crowds of people and if you do not you will not be successful?'

'It depends what you mean by "large crowds". I do not consider a hundred people a day to be a large number.'

'How would you prevent people coming in large numbers?'

'If people came in hundreds and thousands, I would raise the entrance fee.' This raised a laugh in the public gallery.

What it really came down to was money. The well-off residents thought a zoo would lower the tone, and with it the value of their own properties. Oakfield was a private residence and should stay as such.

Dad said that it would be residential, that he and his family were already living there, that it had been empty for over a year before he had bought it, and if the project failed, he would be the only one to be affected.

An estate agent then took the stand. In his view the construction of the new road would cause far more disturbance than the proposed aviary and zoo. There was also talk of an aerodrome being built, and acres of land were already marked out for new housing, and of course there was the new bypass. Compared with disruption on this scale, what was planned at Oakfield was insignificant, he said. Overall he didn't think a zoo at Oakfield would destroy the residential character of Upton and was preferable to a rash of small houses.

At the close of proceedings, the Inspector of Health said that he would visit Oakfield the following day and that anyone who wished to go with him was welcome to do so.

Now all we could do was wait.

Chapter 3

The days and weeks following the appeal hearing were tense and Dad kept everyone busy. We'd come this far, he said, so now we had to 'keep right on to the end of the road'. My father loved all those First World War songs and was always singing them, especially once he learnt to drive, when it seemed he couldn't do one without the other.

It was Mr Buckley who taught him how to change gear, and I would hide in the shrubbery and watch while he practised, lurching down the drive, juddering to a halt, then getting it started again by climbing out and turning the crank handle till the engine stuttered and shuddered into life once more. You didn't need to take a test back then – that only came in in 1934 – but the sound of him crunching through gears was worse than any other noise in the zoo, and it would set off the peacocks, who then set off everyone else.

One day he must have pressed the accelerator instead of the brake, and the next thing I knew the car had veered off the drive and was careering straight for the laurel bush where I was hiding. I ran out just in time and I don't know who was more shocked, Dad or me.

Mr Buckley had come to lend a hand with the building work, turning the loose boxes in the stables, some of which had been used more recently as garages, into secure pens and helping to set up the aviaries. I couldn't do much more than watch, though I have a clear memory of Dad asking me to hand him up nails, one by one, which he then hammered into the wood to keep the netting in place.

Meanwhile Mum was sorting out the domestic side of things. The kitchen was always the warmest place in the house, thanks to a huge old range that took up half the back wall, where all the cooking was done. It was kept going day and night – every few hours the cry would go up, 'Anyone checked the coke?' and woe betide you if you'd let the fire go out. Above the range were two drying racks that extended right across the ceiling and which worked on a pulley system. Winter or summer, these were never empty, and were weighed down either by clothes – from Dad's shirts to Mew's overalls – or later by the damask tablecloths from the café. The back yard was also crisscrossed by washing lines, kept up high with forked wooden props, but even so there never seemed to be enough space.

From the start Dad was determined that everything about the zoo should be 'top notch' – this wasn't a cafeteria or a canteen. The laundry was done in the scullery beside the back door, where there was a huge old copper to heat the water, a big sink and a drain in the floor. Ironing was done in the kitchen using a series of flat irons that would be lined up on the range. When one cooled down, you'd swap it for a hot one.

Backstairs was a labyrinth and each little room had its purpose. Opposite the scullery was where the vegetables were stored: potatoes, carrots, swedes and beetroot. Some things – like onions – were for Mum's stews, which we lived on – but mainly they were for the animals. There were no fridges in those days and this was the coolest of the rooms, with a north-facing wall, so the milk which we'd collect every morning from the farm up the road was also kept there. Food for the carnivores was put in a meat safe in the back yard.

Dry animal feed was stored in a pantry – bins of wheat and crushed oats, and canary and sunflower seeds and millet for the birds. Birds can be as picky as toddlers, so you didn't mix the different seeds; the idea was to ring the changes so they wouldn't get bored. Then there was rice that you'd boil up and mix with honey to give to the smaller herbivores as a treat. The pantry was also where the cod liver oil was kept, an important source of vitamins. Stale or misshapen loaves of bread, which we'd get given free from Dean's bakery, would have holes cut out of the middle and you'd pour a spoonful or two of cod liver oil in and then put the top back on. This was for the bears. Monkeys would get the same, but as sandwiches. Then there would be sacks of peanuts. We couldn't afford many hard-shelled nuts, even though that's what parrots would live on in the wild – things like Brazils were much too dear.

The pantry was also where we bred mealworms, the larvae of the mealworm beetle. Monkeys would do anything if they knew a few juicy mealworms would be their reward. These lived in a dustbin among layers of crumpled newspaper, where the beetles would lay their eggs, and when they'd hatched you'd shake the mealworms out. When I got a bit older my job was to feed them with rolled oats and water, making sure that the lid was firmly back on when I'd finished.

One room was always kept locked and only my mother and Muriel had the key. This was the larder, where special things were kept – like bananas and grapes and other delicacies when we had any. The south- and west-facing walls of the kitchen garden were lined with espalier peach, nectarine and medlars, which Granddad cared for like they were his children, though they only cropped in a good summer. There was a marble counter in the larder, and here Muriel would do all her cutting up. I remember standing behind her, my arms round her waist, pleading for 'just one taste', and sometimes she took pity on me. The stock of tea and coffee for the café was also kept there and the shelves were stacked high with jars of Granny's home-made jam: rhubarb, gooseberry and plum, as well as lemon curd, which was my favourite. I remember her making crab apple jelly, when the boiled fruit would be strung up in muslin 'nets' in her kitchen in the lodge, with a tin bath underneath, so that you'd hear the drip, drip, dripping all through the night.

Our supply of honey was also kept under lock and key. A local man was allowed to keep his beehives in the orchard and we'd get some of their honey in return. Honey was always very precious and would be doled out to sick animals by the teaspoonful.

The fruit from the orchard was kept in a brick hut set half into the ground in the kitchen garden, next to the potting shed. Inside it was completely dark, with no light except when the door was open. Being below ground like this made it frost-proof. You went down two steps and on either side were racks of slatted wooden shelves where apples and pears were carefully placed so as not to touch each other. The orchard at

Oakfield was large – nearly four acres – and, if we were careful, Granddad explained, the apples would last us through till the spring, but only if they didn't touch, because if one rotted, they would all soon be gone. Beneath the shelves were sand boxes where potatoes, beetroot and carrots were buried until they were needed. That apple store is still there to this day.

On 13 March 1931, a little over a month after the hearing, Dad got a telegram from his solicitor saying the appeal had been granted and the zoo could now open, subject to an agreement being reached with the City of Chester, who could stipulate 'reasonable conditions'.

There were no great celebrations. There was no more money and with April less than three weeks away Dad knew that the chance of the zoo opening in time for the Easter holiday was zero.

'Nil desperandum,' he said. 'With any luck we'll get the go-ahead in time for Whitsun.' Seven weeks after Easter – ten weeks after the telegram – it should have been possible. But luck, it seemed, had deserted us and the zoo's detractors were not about to make it easy. To all intents and purposes, they were the City of Chester.

In the meantime the solicitor was working hard on Dad's behalf. Two weeks after

Easter he was told that the town clerk was away and so nothing could be done until his return. On 1 May Chester town-planning committee met. They reiterated that they did not want to enter into any agreement with Mr Mottershead. However, pressure must somehow have been brought to bear. A reply dated 13 May finally arrived from the town clerk. Mr Mottershead could open the zoo subject to: 1) the type of animals being limited to those already described in previous correspondence; 2) the estate should not be used as an amusement park, racing track or public dance hall; and 3) no animals were to be kept within a distance of a hundred feet from the existing road.

This necessitated the purchase of an additional strip of land between the road and the estate, which would have to be securely enclosed, but which couldn't be used for animals. (First it was used as a children's playground and later became a self-service café.) Somehow my dad managed to get a further mortgage of £350 to pay for the land and the fencing.

Of all the conditions, the most damaging in the long term was the last: the zoo was allowed 'no advertisement, sign or notice-board which can be seen from the road above-mentioned'. Only a small sign at the entrance to the estate would be permitted, which meant the lodge, which was a good twenty-five yards from the road and completely invisible to any passing car. This would remain a problem for a very long time. For many years, the night before bank holidays, Dad and his friends would have to go out and hang temporary posters under the official road signs on the Chester bypass. The police turned a blind eye as long as they were taken down shortly afterwards.

For several weeks, in between his gardening tasks, Granddad had been busy making a series of concrete ponds, linked up by underground pipes so that the water was always moving. These would be for goldfish and rudd, he explained. But the first pond he'd made had been much bigger – more of a miniature lake – and was right by the entrance, opposite the lodge where he and Granny lived. The clay he dug out became a kind of hillock and, while he worked, I played, making mud castles and using twigs for flag poles and leaves for flags. This one wouldn't be lined with concrete, he explained. It would always have a mud bottom, because by the time the summer came, where I was playing would be deep water, home to water birds, including flamingos, and they'd need the worms and insects that would live there. By then the hillock would be covered with plants and flowers, with reeds growing at the water's edge. It would be the first thing visitors would see when they arrived at the zoo, so it was important to make a bit of a splash. And the last job Granddad did at night was to light oil lamps around it to keep the foxes at bay.

The new arrivals settled in very quickly: two barnacle geese, as well as Mandarin and Carolina ducks so colourful they looked like painted wooden toys bobbing about on the water, then some Muscovy ducks from Mexico that were not as handsome – to me they looked like black and white chickens – but who were soon bossing the others about.

Although Granny had never liked animals, ducks didn't seem to count. So every morning she would gather up what was left in the breadbin and climb to the top of the muddy hillock and throw it to them, scattering it far and wide to make sure the Muscovys didn't get it all. She was a great one for ritual, and she fed them every morning at the same time, and most days I would wander down and watch her before going in for a slice of bread and lemon curd. Then, if I was good, and she had the time, she would let me brush her hair.

Granny never left the house without being 'properly dressed', and even though the pond was only across the drive, it made no difference. 'You never know who might pass by,' she explained. When she was at home – or in the small garden behind the lodge – she wore a wraparound pinafore made of printed cotton cretonne over whatever she was wearing, but 'properly dressed' meant no pinny, a jacket and a hat. It wasn't just because she was old-fashioned – though she was; everyone wore something on their heads in those days, men and women, though feeding the ducks only warranted Granny's second-best hat.

So one May morning, with everything smelling fresh and glistening after a night of rain, I set off along the drive, skipping and hopping as I usually did. And there was Granny, already standing on the hillock, throwing her crusts to the squabbling birds. She was like a pillar, dressed top to toe in brown, her skirt reaching down to her ankles. Then, as I spotted a Muscovy duck trying to edge out a Mandarin by nipping his tail feathers, she started to slip, then the slip turned into a slither, and the next thing I knew my grandmother was flat on her back, sliding slowly but inevitably into the water. She didn't yell or scream – that would have been undignified – and there was nothing I could do but watch open-mouthed as the ducks parted to let her sail through. And then she disappeared. For a moment all I could see was her second-best hat floating on the surface ... and then a flurry of water, and there she was, her lovely white hair now caked with mud. She tried to climb out, but her skirts were sodden and pulled her down.

I turned and ran back up the drive, calling my grandfather's name – I knew where he was, as I'd said hello on my way. The hat was eventually retrieved – as of course was Granny – but I never saw her wear it again.

A week or so before the zoo was due to open Dad disappeared up to Liverpool with Mr Buckley. A mixed shipment of animals and birds from Nigeria had come in on the Blue Funnel Line, a freight shipping company that did the West Africa route, owned by a Liverpool family called Holt. The Holts had a near-monopoly and everyone wanted to keep in with them, including Nigerian chiefs, who would present them with gifts of animals which, as the Holts didn't want them, would get passed on to people who did, in this case my father. I don't know how Dad first met Miss Esther Holt, but she seemed to be the one who organised this side of things and from then on we were first on her list.

Among this shipment in May 1931 were two young chimpanzees. Perhaps Dad knew this before he went but didn't want to raise my hopes, because ever since we'd had to leave Babs behind at Shavington, I had been pestering him to get one. To me, a zoo wasn't a proper zoo without a chimp.

John and Mary – named by the sailors – were still infants when they arrived at Oak-field. They were little more than a year old and must have been taken from their mother when they were babies and were lucky to have survived. Most likely she would have been killed for bush meat, and they would have ended up at a local market – chimpanzees have been kept as pets in Africa for hundreds of years. And now fate had brought them to me.

I can remember even now how excited I was when Mr Buckley's car pulled up and Dad told me to come and see what he'd got in the back. It was packed with cages full of animals, but when I saw the chimps I jumped up and down. I couldn't believe it! Our very own chimpanzees!

However, it was soon clear there was a problem. They were ill, both of them – eyes streaming, coughing and sneezing, cuddling up to each other just like human babies. They must have caught something, Dad said, from the sailors on the ship. But what a human, even a human baby, can throw off in a few days, or even a few weeks, can be life-threatening to a chimp. Mew took control – she had looked after Babs when she'd been ill and knew what to do. She made cots for them both from cardboard boxes and kept them in her room. But when Dad said they had to go into their cages for the opening day, Mew wasn't happy.

'They're still not well, Dad, and the last thing they need is contact with more germs.'

'I'm sorry, Mew, but I need them on view. Visitors have to know we've got them. You heard what June said. It's not a proper zoo without chimps.' And after all, he added, it was June not December.

My sister made their cage as comfortable as she could and gave them each a hand-knitted blanket to curl up in. Dad promised that no one would be allowed to handle them, and in that he was as good as his word. Until the day of the opening they stayed with my sister. As Mary wasn't as ill as John, Mew would let me cradle her while she fed her sick brother from a bottle. Mary herself was well enough to take a mug, which she had learnt how to use on the ship.

The opening date was now only a few days away – 10 June 1931. Following the solicitor's advice, there would be no trumpet-blowing, no razzmatazz. Dad should do everything possible to avoid any ill feeling, he'd said. We decided on a trial run, when just friends came, people like the Buckleys, and the Lightfoots and Mr Eaton. Then we had the official opening. I can remember being so excited. I wore my best summer frock with white socks and sandals and Granny brushed my hair till it shone. She was in charge of the pay box, a little wooden hut beside the lodge, and was 'properly dressed', wearing a new straw hat. The cost was 1/- for adults and 6d for children. And our luck did now seem to be holding. Dad had been given a pelican, called Pelly. He'd been somebody's pet so was friendly right from the start and seemed quite happy just wandering around. As pelicans go he wasn't that big though he seemed enormous to me as he was the first one I'd seen. Pelly lived on herrings and Dad taught me how to feed them to him one by one. You had to hold them right at the end of their tails, because on Pelly's beak there was a hook that could give you a nasty cut. The flamingos, which Dad had despaired of ever arriving, had turned up two days before. They spent half the time standing on one red leg, looking superior, the other half they spent with their heads underwater looking for shrimps, which is what gives them that pink colour. As Granddad's pond didn't run to shrimps, they got given them in a dish, which had to be put underwater as that was the only way they would eat.

The day of the trial run had been hot, not a cloud in the sky. Tables had been laid on the lawn in front of the big house for teas. There were striped deck chairs and parasols. Inside, the tables were laid with starched damask tablecloths. Mum had been up half the night finishing the baking, and piles of bread and butter were stacked up under muslin squares weighed down with stones at the corners to keep any flies off.

In the end the opening day was half sunny,

half showery, but it didn't really matter. The peacocks spread their tails under the cedar, looking as if they'd always been there. In the courtyard even Adam and Eve looked better. The last few weeks had seen the end of their winter coats and the new fur underneath looked healthy and glossy and they even seemed to enjoy the rain.

Nobody came. Well, only a handful – nothing like the crowds Dad had been hoping for, although there'd been plenty of enquiries in the weeks running up, with people coming to the house asking when the zoo was going to open. But there was one good thing to happen that day. Dad had made sure that the two local newspapers had been invited and he treated the reporters as guests of honour. He took them everywhere, explained everything – he let them hold the monkeys, things that ordinary visitors wouldn't be allowed to do. One had brought his children and they were given a ride on Minnie the tapir, who lived across from the bears. Only the chimps – the other side of the bears – were out of bounds, though visitors could look at them. Mary was now getting better – she was up at the front of the cage, intrigued by the people who'd come to see her. She would run to the back of the pen and take John's arm and make noises to persuade him to go with her. But he wouldn't. He stayed curled up at the back, and just kept on coughing.

Two days later Dad burst into the kitchen, where Mum was laying the table for lunch, waving a newspaper. 'We've done it, Lizzie!' he said. 'We've damn well done it. And if this isn't one in the eye for the killjoys, I don't know what is. A knockout blow, I would say,' and then, leaving a copy on the table, he rushed out to find Granddad.

Muriel began to read it out loud while Mum pulled up a chair and I sat on her lap and listened.

I have the cuttings in front of me now – in fact there were two of them, both long. In spite of the rain, in spite of the delays in getting the enclosures finished, the *Chester Observer* wrote, 'Oakfield is a veritable garden of Eden.' The grounds were 'a feast of colour and a delight to the eye' and all the animals were mentioned. 'The only large animal being a tapir, commonly known as the water elephant.' It ended, 'A more delightful afternoon's excursion is hard to imagine,' and it gave the telephone number.

The *Chester Chronicle* said, 'The two predominant impressions from a walk round the Oakfield are the extraordinarily natural fitness of the premises for the purposes it is to serve, and that the zoo is going to be a boon to the people of Chester and a very wide area.'

I had never seen Dad so jaunty; his moustache seemed to twist up at the ends and

Mew said he had grown six inches taller. After glowing reports like these – and in today's parlance they were the equivalent of five-star reviews, with not one negative word – they would be fighting to get in, he said. The question would be, how to cope with the queues!

It didn't happen. Luckily Dad had rigged up a bell on a rope which visitors pulled if there was nobody there, and from then on Granny stayed inside the lodge, only coming out when someone turned up, which wasn't very often. But we stayed open. Dad was insistent. From ten in the morning until dusk every day. The costs were the same whether we opened or not, he said. The animals still had to be fed and kept clean, and the message had to get through. 'We are here, and we are here to stay.'

The next month there was a group visit from the Chester Natural Science Society. This was particularly important. For the most part, the members were people who came from the ranks of Chester's well-to-do, the privileged classes he hoped might be persuaded to invest in such a worthwhile cause.

Their report, published in the local press, was all that Dad could have wished for, and again he was convinced they would spell the end of our troubles, both financially and in terms of how the zoo was seen locally.

'It had not been fully realised that Mr Mottershead is making a determined effort to create for us a real zoological collection on the lines of those in existence in cities like Dublin and Bristol, but on a smaller scale ... Mr Mottershead is a lover of both plants and animals and is taking the greatest care in placing the enclosures to preserve the beauty of the gardens.'

The report from the *Chester Chronicle* said, 'The zoo is not a place where the animals vie for popularity with side shows and amusements but it is a place where the student of animal life can find much to interest him.' The reporter from the *Observer* said that at first he had been sceptical. He had wanted to see 'how the gardens and surroundings had been affected by the introduction of birds and beasts and to see how these creatures were kept'.

His mind was soon set at rest, he said. 'Mr Mottershead cares for his beautiful and grotesque charges as highly and as lovingly as possible...' But loving care only goes so far.

The article was accompanied by a photograph – the members of the society together with our family. I'm sitting beside Mum and between me and Dad is Mary, who has one arm on Dad's knee and one on mine. Mary the chimpanzee, the reporter wrote, was the most popular exhibit in the zoo. This time there was no sign nor mention of John, because John had died.

Mew had done everything she could, but chimpanzees are very susceptible to respiratory infections. Simple colds can turn into pneumonia, and until antibiotics came along after the war, pneumonia and TB were responsible for the high number of deaths – 60 per cent – among all the great apes in captivity.

I had never had time to grow close to John. He had been with us for not much longer than a month, six weeks at the most, and I'm not sure I had even held him properly because, with him so being ill, Mew wouldn't have allowed me to. But Mary was different. Mew had handed her over to me because she'd had to concentrate on John. And, who knows, perhaps Mary became needier because she'd lost her twin, her companion since they were born and with whom she'd gone through all the terrible things that had happened. I can still remember what her fur felt like on my cheek when we cuddled. Her forehead was like a rough shelf and she'd lean her head on mine and stare into my eyes. We would stare at each other. Her eyes were like the colour of toffees and were full of intelligence, even then.

Every evening Muriel would make her up a warm drink of milk, with a spoonful of sticky Radio Malt stirred in to give her extra vitamins, and I would be allowed to give it to her. I remember how there would always be drops of milk still sticking to the sparse white hairs on her stubborn little chin. The palms of her hands, holding the enamel mug, were still pink in those days – they got darker as she got older – and her fingers would clench and unclench the handle as she drank.

And so that's how our friendship started, and she and I became great companions. She got used to being put in her cage during the day and it never really seemed to bother her – she was very placid and calm by nature. She was always as gentle with other children as she was with me. Even when visitors were around, she would be taken out though she would usually stay in Muriel's arms. But once the visitors had gone it was different and we would be left on our own. Like any human toddler, she loved to copy. I had a doll's pram and she and I would take it in turns to push it across the grass. We would chatter away, and I don't remember ever feeling that she didn't understand. She had a special hoot that she made when she saw me. It was her sound for 'Hello, June!' – and it was just for me. She had special noises for lots of things, most of which I understood. I learnt to copy her – just as she would copy me.

It wasn't until the 60s when Jane Goodall 'shocked' the scientific world with her revelations that chimps had their own language and could use tools. Until then, being able to use tools was proof that man was different from animals. I knew that Mary could use tools before Jane Goodall was born. When Dad taught her how to use a screwdriver, there was no stopping her.

Looking back at those first months now, I don't know how we survived. It wasn't just our family who had to be fed, it was the animals too. There weren't that many in those early days, but even so. Not a week would go by without Dad hearing of a sailor who'd come back with a monkey he couldn't keep and who'd sold it to a pet shop, or an old lady who'd died leaving a parrot without a home – parrots live to a very ripe age. At least there were no wages to pay – we had no staff unless you counted Granddad, who worked for nothing. In fact his and Granny's pension was probably what we lived on. By now it had risen to 10/- a week. The money Dad had raised from the mortgage had all gone on the land so he sold the remaining parcels of land he'd held on to at Shavington to furnish the house, which, apart from what we had brought with us from Shavington, had been totally empty when we got there.

But, just like the damask tablecloths, he knew that it had to look the part. This wasn't furniture for upstairs, which no one but us would see, this was for the rooms used by the public and well-to-do visitors. So he went to an auction at a big country house somewhere in the Wirral, near Birkenhead, and came back with enough things to make downstairs look properly furnished. He bought a large circular table, which is still there, and a beautiful walnut sideboard, which went in the morning room and where the cutlery and crockery for the café was kept. I remember there were two pheasants carved on the doors, hanging upside down. He also bought three stuffed animal heads, including a bear's and an antelope's, the kind of things big-game hunters might have as trophies, which is probably just what they were. They went up in the outer hall and the glass eyes stared at you every time you went in. Then there were two Victorian glass display cases, one with a stuffed snowy owl, the other a bird of paradise whose amazing feathers took up most of the space. These went in the café. Finally there were two big oil paintings, also Victorian probably, of a whiskery gentleman and his wife, which hung side by side in the inner hall.

Once the main staircase had been boarded up (we used the back stairs from the servants' quarters to get to our bedrooms), I used to sit there in the dark. It was somewhere I could hide to avoid doing jobs I hated, like the washing up, and I'd listen to Dad giving visitors various versions of who these two portraits were. Sometimes they were his ancestors, sometimes my mum's, sometimes they were previous owners of Oakfield. The truth was, he didn't have a clue who they were.

I had turned five a week after the zoo opened and started school the following September. Just like Muriel had in Crewe, Mum decided I would go to the convent. And just as with Muriel, it was my Atkinson grandparents who paid the fees. But it was still an expensive decision because of the uniform, which you had to buy from the official outfitters in Chester. It consisted of a navy-blue gymslip, white blouse and blue tie, as well as a gabardine coat or a blazer in the summer and a blue felt hat. Like any child, I seemed to be always growing and I know that over the years it must have cost my parents a fortune. But they never bought anything that wasn't obligatory, like the panoramic school photos that were taken every year – I never had one of those.

It wasn't just that Mum thought I'd get a better education with the nuns, she was worried about the bad feeling there was in Upton and thought that if I went to the village school there could be problems. Even going to the convent in Chester, Dad said that I was never to talk about things that went on, never to say anything except that everything was a great success and encourage my friends to come and visit with their families.

The reality was I didn't have any friends for quite a long time, until I got to know girls who lived in the country, like Nancy and Margaret Lloyd (though neither of them were in my class) who were farmers' daughters and who understood about animals, and Zena Law whose mum ran The Grosvenor Arms, a pub on the Duke of Westminster's estate. Even then we never visited each other's houses until we were old enough to have bicycles because we came from different directions. I only had one friend who lived within walking distance, a girl called June Hinde, and she never came to the zoo because her parents were well-off and had signed the petition. When she did eventually come she was frightened by things that to me were quite ordinary – Minnie the tapir wandering around and Pelly demanding his tea at the back door and Rob Rob the blue and red macaw who seemed to spend half his life in the kitchen gouging chunks out of the chairs.

At least at Oakfield I had Mary. The bus stop into Chester was in the village, and so Granny would walk me up there in the morning and collect me in the afternoons. Once I'd rushed upstairs and taken off my uniform, I'd go down, ask Muriel to let Mary out and then we'd play. If it was raining or cold we'd stay in the house. Mary loved dressing up – and she particularly loved hats. Nowadays, dressing up a chimp in human clothes would be seen as terrible, but it was Mary who loved it, mainly because she just wanted to be like me. I became Mary's translator. If other people didn't understand what she wanted, I'd explain for her. Her language was our language, one that no one else could fully understand – not even Muriel – a combination of grunts and gestures. Anything I did, she wanted to do too, and I remember teaching her to plait a rope, though for once she didn't do it as well as me.

To me, all this was normal life. I didn't know what other children did when they got home. You didn't know what other fathers did or what their jobs entailed. Shirley Fraser's father was a doctor, but she never mentioned the people who visited her dad's surgery or what their illnesses were. So why should I talk about the latest consignment of monkeys, or crested cranes, or the difference between a boa constrictor and a python?

Chapter 4

My father was an early convert to the value of free publicity. Soon every new arrival at the zoo would be announced in the local press, usually accompanied by a picture of a 'young visitor' – me. When I wasn't suitable, for whatever reason, it would be Muriel who would just be captioned as 'a visitor', without the 'young', though by any standards she was hardly old. In 1932 Mew was sixteen and very beautiful. It shone through the dirt and grime involved in cleaning out cages, sluicing down yards, mucking out and the rest of the daily life of our zoo. She had perfect skin and bone structure that nothing could disguise.

Dad was soon coming up with schemes to broaden the range of visitors and keep them coming back. That first summer he ran a photography competition. It was for the best 'snap' of an animal or bird taken in the gardens. The first prize was a season ticket and a 'folding' camera. When you opened it up a concertina bellows popped out and the lens was at the end. It was one step up from a Box Brownie and was donated by a friend of Dad's called Mr Rose who sold them in his shop, so it would have been publicity for him too. Cameras were expensive in those days – this one would have cost about £16 – and for anyone interested in photography it would be worth paying the shilling entrance fee for the chance to win it, not to mention the chance of having your photo featured in the local paper. The ten runners-up also got season tickets. It was all clever thinking on Dad's part. Just to enter the competition, they would need to buy a ticket.

There were literally hundreds of entries. I remember Dad sitting with Mew in the housekeeper's room going through them all, each one numbered and labelled. And all this for the cost of a camera which he'd got free anyway.

The prize-giving was in September. Dad gave me the job of disc jockey – though I don't think the word existed back then – putting records on the gramophone in my mother's bedroom, which were played over a loudspeaker at the front of the house where everyone congregated, while Mew and my mum served up the teas on the lawn. Paying customers were still few and far between, and as this was a 'do', refreshments were provided free. We seemed to provide an awful lot of free teas to people during those first few summers, which we noticed more than we would later as we were counting every penny. But, as was drummed into me over and over, with our collection of animals being so small, we had to make a huge effort and be very nice to our visitors and that meant giving them cakes and bread with plenty of butter. There could be no skimping.

Dad's plan to raise money from local people appeared to be working. In October 1931 Chester Zoological Gardens became a limited liability company, with a nominal capital of £5,000. He knew at the time it wasn't enough, but what was he to do? Backers included Captain Rogers, who had recently started up a small zoo on the Rosemont Estate in Mossley Hill, Liverpool; Mr Lightfoot, a grocer in Chester who lived in a large house in Mill Lane in Upton, who'd given evidence on Dad's behalf at the inquiry; and Mr Brookshaw, an old friend from Shavington. But these weren't the gentry that Dad was hoping for.

Then, in the spring of 1932, Dr English got in touch. The zoo at Shavington was losing too much money, he said, so it was going to be closed and the animals sold off. Any he couldn't get rid of, he said, he'd give to Dad. Babs was ill with some kind of respiratory infection, so she came. There was Lulu the ring-tailed lemur, who was really a pet and didn't get on with other monkeys. Then there was a Tasmanian devil, a vicious marsupial with stripes on its back going from side to side, that looked like a dog and whom I absolutely hated. Luckily he didn't stay long as Dad didn't like him either and exchanged him for something else. In terms of birds, the parrots, lorikeets and budgerigars had all been bought; we inherited just a pair of griffon vultures. The saddest was a polar bear named Punch. Polar bears were valuable, but Punch looked so old and bedraggled that nobody was prepared to buy him, so Dad agreed to give him a home, even though at that point there was nowhere suitable for him to go.

Punch had been bought by Dr English from Bostock and Wombwell's travelling menagerie and, until arriving at Shavington, had spent his entire life confined in a cage that was small enough to be put in a van, being lugged back and forth across England from Norwich, where the menagerie was based. Life didn't get much better at Shavington, Dad said, because Punch had been kept in a corrugated iron shed. When he arrived at Oakfield he was put in the old blacksmith's shop, where horses used to be shoed. Dad found him an old enamel bath, but it wasn't nearly big enough for him to get into. Luckily he didn't have to stay there for long.

Mum's brother, Christopher, Uncle Kit, came down from Westmorland for a holiday, arriving on his motorcycle. He was quite unlike her other brother, Uncle Billy, who never left the farm. Uncle Kit was a bit of a 'tearaway' and would go dirt-track racing at Belle Vue. Within a couple of weeks he and my dad had dug out a brand-new pen for Punch against the back wall of the kitchen garden. The earth sides were strengthened with reinforced concrete, the reinforcement being an old brass bedstead that someone had thrown out. Above the ground, the fence was just iron posts covered with chicken wire. He had a 'den' at the back which could be shut off with a metal grille, so the main pen could be cleaned out when he wasn't in it. They also incorporated a concrete pool that was big enough for a soak rather than a swim, but Punch never used it anyway. According to the story Dad would tell visitors, having lived in captivity all his life, Punch didn't know what it was for.

Before he'd arrived, I'd known what to expect because of Fox's Glacier Mints. But I was very disappointed. Compared to the label on the sweet jar in the village shop – a shiny white bear standing on a blue block of ice – poor Punch was more of a dirty yellow, like slush compared to freshly fallen snow. He was lacklustre not only in his looks, but in his attitude to life. You'd say now that he was depressed – because he didn't look after himself and never seemed to move out of one corner of his pen, spending most of the time asleep, or pretending to be. I felt so sorry for him. There he was, all on his own, with no one to talk to. I wanted him to be like my other animal friends, who'd come over and listen when I talked to them.

Punch became my biggest challenge. Every day after school I'd pay him a visit and chat, just as I'd done with the bears we'd had in Shavington. Mew had a book with pictures called Wildlife of the World which she would let me look at, so I would tell him all about the Arctic Ocean and how cold it was up there, and about the icebergs. I told him that Dad was sure to find him a wife soon and then he wouldn't be so lonely. First he took no notice of me at all, but I didn't give up. I went to see him every day, sat on the ground by his fence and just talked, about what I'd done at school, how much I hated it and how cross Sister Imelda would get with my class, saying we 'looked like a lot of Cheshire cows'. And how I didn't really have any friends except Mary and him.

It took a while for him to learn to trust me and to realise that I wasn't an ordinary visitor like the rest. I made sure I spoke gently and in a steady way, and so gradually he got used to my visits. He began to raise his head and look in my direction at the sound of my voice. A few days more and he stood up. A few days after that and he lumbered over to where I was sitting and looked at me talking to him on the other side of the bars. From then on, whenever he heard me coming, he would come over and lean against the wall and just listen. I never gave him anything to eat, I just gave him companionship and made him feel a little less lonely.

In the early days, when the animals were all in pens in the stable block, the non-dangerous ones would be let out to wander around the courtyard once the visitors had left. The gate that led out into the garden would be shut so they couldn't get out. One of those with the freedom of the courtyard was Minnie the tapir, who the monkeys used to tease mercilessly. They were very naughty, creeping up behind to nip her or tweak her tail. Or just dancing about in front of her then scampering away when she made a lunge. They always got away because she couldn't move that fast.

A tapir is about the same size as a pig, but with longer legs and a prehensile, downward-pointing snout that roots out food from the ground. In fact its closest relative is the rhinoceros. Tapirs are herbivores, so before going to see her I would look in the orchard for windfall apples, which she loved, and in the winter there'd be medlars from the kitchen garden. Her usual diet was mostly leaves and small branches.

One day – it was probably May or June – I was informed that my parents were going out to a dinner party and so I would be staying the night with Granny and Granddad at the lodge. This was very unusual. Although Dad was always socialising, meeting people who he thought might become investors, he always went alone, while Mum stayed at the house with us. But this was obviously something that had been planned for a long time because Granny had made Mum a special dress. I'd seen her sewing it on an old Singer treadle machine. It was a blue, silky material and I thought it looked beautiful. It was going to be very smart – the guest of honour was Lady So-and-So. But the night before I had heard raised voices coming from Mum's bedroom. For the first year in Oakfield I had slept in her room, but by then my bed had been moved into Mew's next door.

'I won't feel comfortable with those kind of people, George, you know I won't,' my mother had said. 'I'm not their class.'

'Class has nothing to do with it, Lizzie. You're as good as they are any day, and I won't have you saying otherwise.'

'But you're used to them.'

'I wasn't a year ago. You have to start sometime and it might as well be now. I can't do any of this without you, you know, and what kind of a thank you is that for my mother for all the work she's done?'

In the end she was persuaded. The hot water for the bath had been heated specially and Granny was coming over to do her hair and I was then going back with her to the lodge.

I suppose I must have felt left out. But, whatever the reason, I decided I would hold my own dinner party, with Minnie as the guest of honour, not that I knew what a dinner party was. So once the zoo was closed, and Mum and Dad were upstairs getting dolled up, I went to the apple store and collected as many carrots as I could hold, took them into the pantry and cut out the bad bits. I found some leftover bread and butter and smeared it liberally with lemon curd – that was for me. I then took two plates and made my way to the courtyard. For once Mum hadn't done her rounds, so I think the animals were restless. They had all been locked up for the night, but Minnie was still wandering around. She was never any trouble and often stayed out, just snuffling. Once visitors had left, her pen door stayed open so she could come and go as she pleased. She had always been very independent-minded.

I sat down and put the plates beside me on the first step of the spiral staircase leading up to the turret. It was wider than the rest and more like a little landing. I then called Minnie to come and have her supper. When she smelled the carrots and saw how many there were, she began wolfing them down. Suddenly there was a commotion in the monkey cages behind us – a few of the monkeys had started a fight – and then Mary started shaking her wire mesh and whooping.

Minnie was always wary of anything to do with the monkeys and she bolted. Not back to her pen, but straight on the way she was pointing, up the spiral staircase. One minute she was there beside me, snaffling the carrots, the next she'd vanished from sight. I ran up after her, calling her name, telling her not to be so silly, that it was only the monkeys making trouble and that they were safely locked up so she had nothing to worry about. By the time I found her she had nearly reached the top and she was stuck. She couldn't move up or down.

I didn't know what to do. I hadn't done anything really wrong. I didn't need special permission to go into the courtyard, there was just a latch, not a key. And I was always giving Minnie carrots, though admittedly not the great heap I had got for her that evening.

I knew there was nothing for it but to tell Dad.

He and my mother hadn't shared a bedroom since Shavington – they each had their own – so I went to Dad's.

'Minnie's stuck,' I told him.

'What do you mean, stuck?' He was busy fiddling with his bow tie in the wardrobe mirror and didn't look at me or notice I'd been crying.

'In the turret.'

At that he turned round. 'In the turret?'

'At the top... It wasn't my fault, it was the monkeys...'

Giving his bow tie a last pat, he put his hand on my shoulder and said, 'Right, young lady, you'll have to show me.'

When we got to the courtyard I pointed up at the turret and there was Minnie's snout, poking out of the window, just like the princess I'd always imagined it had been built for.

He raced up the steps two at a time and then I heard my name being called.

'I need you to fetch Mew,' he said.

'She's not here.'

'Well where is she?'

'Out collecting insects.' I'd seen her disappearing up the drive with her butterfly net. There was always a need for insects for the birds.

'Then fetch your mother. Tell her I need her. Chop chop.'

I ran back to the house, through the garden door and up the back stairs to Mum's room at the front, overlooking the garden. She was sitting at her dressing table, with Granny standing behind fussing with her hair.

'Dad says he needs you,' I blurted out.

'I don't know,' my grandmother said, 'it's always rush, rush, rush with him. You can tell your father from me that another five minutes won't hurt.'

I didn't move.

'Well, be off, child. Else he'll be honking that car horn and setting off the peacocks.'

'But he's not in the car!'

'Not in the car?' This was my mother's voice, and she turned round to look at me.

'He's in the turret!'

'What's he doing there?' Granny looked round too and for the first time they saw my tear-stained face.

'He's with Minnie,' I said. 'She's stuck. That's why he needs you.'

Mum was up from her stool and out of the door in seconds. She was wearing new shoes, the sort that shouldn't be worn in the garden, and as she ran, her dress caught between her legs.

'I'm not convinced she's stuck,' Dad said to Mum when we got there. 'She's just contrary and has decided she doesn't want to go any further. But I think I know how we can do it. You go up by the other staircase, Lizzie, and see if you can get through.'

Then he turned his attention to me. 'Whereas you, young lady, are coming with me. And bring that with you.' On the floor of the courtyard were two china plates and an uneaten lemon curd sandwich.

When we reached the top Minnie was blocking the way. We heard Mum's muffled voice saying she couldn't get any further because the door was bolted from the other side. It had been the groom's flat, and later Mew would live there, but back then it was just a storeroom.

'Right,' Dad said and lifted me up, setting me astride Minnie's back. I'd often ridden on her before so she was used to bearing my weight. 'Now just wriggle your way across and slide down over her head.' So I did, giving her a scratch behind her ears as I went, to let her know everything was all right.

'Now, listen carefully. Stand a bit back – and hold that sandwich out in front of you, but don't let her have it. I'm going to lift her back legs up one at a time. And when she moves, you move. Keep her interested, but keep the sandwich out of her reach. And keep talking to her. The trick is to keep her calm.'

And so I did. Telling Minnie how nice Granny's lemon curd was, and how she would never taste anything so delicious, and how it was a great treat and much nicer than carrots, which she could have every day. Her snout came out and wiggled around, sniffing the lemon curd. And then she moved. And I took half a step towards her.

'Good work,' said Dad. And so it went on, with him pulling her back legs down one stair at a time. I don't know how many there were, but the turret was the tallest thing in the courtyard, double the height of anything else. It must have gone on for the best part of an hour.

Once Minnie reached the ground and saw daylight she couldn't get out fast enough and made straight for her pen, and Dad clanged the gate shut behind her. A few minutes later Mum reappeared carrying an apple – one of the last of Granddad's winter store – which she gave to Minnie. Her dress was torn at the hem, her stockings were laddered, she was covered in white powder where the distemper on the walls had rubbed off and her hair was all over the place. That night they were going nowhere.

There's a saying that there's no such thing as bad publicity. And perhaps it's true. For in July that year the zoo made headlines in the national press for the first time, but not in the way anyone would have expected or wanted, not even Dad. It was a week after our first 'gramophone concert', which he had hoped would become a weekly event. That only got a small mention in the local paper, but MONKEY COMMITS SUICIDE was everywhere, from *The Times* to the *Daily Sketch*. It had happened in full view of visitors. According to the various reports, one of the rhesus monkeys, which we called macaques, had been seen gnawing off a length of rope, which he then tied onto a branch. With the other end, he made a noose with a slipknot, then put this over his head and jumped, breaking his neck and dying instantly.

Even from this distance, it's a shocking story, and over the next few months the debate simmered in the press, both through letters to the editor and in editorials. The issue was simple: was it a deliberate suicide? Had this monkey had enough of life in the zoo and decided to end it? Some people used it to attack the principle of keeping wild animals in captivity. Dad even had a letter from the famous anthropologist Solly Zuckerman, but the truth is that it was just a tragic accident. It wasn't until years later that I saw a photograph of this poor monkey hanging from the noose that he'd made, looking horribly like a human. It distressed me then and it distresses me now.

But the tragedy of this 'suicidal' monkey put Chester Zoo on the map. People from much further afield who didn't take the local paper read about it and it got them talking, exactly the kind of people Dad had hoped to interest in the first place. Although local opposition to the zoo had mainly faded away, at least among ordinary folk who lived in ordinary houses in the village, people with money – like Sir John Frost and his other well-off Chester cronies – were not about to be proved wrong. Dad had done everything he could. He'd given talks at village halls and sent out circulars setting out his view for the future of the zoo: how larger enclosures, where visitors could see animals in 'natural' surroundings, were better for everybody – views that were already being put into practice at Whipsnade, London Zoo's country park in Bedfordshire – and how it would be a valuable amenity for the people of Cheshire. He got no takers.

The company Dad had set up to run the zoo a year earlier was already heavily in debt and he knew he had to come up with another solution or the bailiffs would move in. As he had sold his fields in Shavington, the little bit of rent he'd got from those had gone. Meanwhile the interest on the mortgage continued to build up, and the investors in the company needed to see a return on their money. Above all, the animals had to be fed. It was a financial disaster. In the two years since the zoo had opened there had been fewer people through the gate than in the last six months at Shavington.

The one thing he didn't want to do was to turn Oakfield into an amusement park. Even though that would have been the easiest solution, it went against everything the zoo stood for, against everything he and Mum and Granddad had fought for.

But while this was going on, Dad's relentless pursuit of potential investors had led him to the next level up of landowners. They weren't interested in helping Dad make money particularly, but they were interested in animals. What about turning it into a non-profit-making society? And so, in September 1932, the Chester Zoological Society was founded. These were not bank managers and flour-mill owners, these were baronets and even peers of the realm. The vice-presidents included the Duchess of Westminster and the 2nd Viscount Lever-hulme, a very well-known industrialist and philanthropist, like his father before him. Their first project was to publish an account of the animals, birds and reptiles usually found in zoos, about each species' natural habitat, food and how it differed from the food they had to eat in captivity. It would also double as a guide to Chester Zoo. But before long it became obvious that there wouldn't be a zoo to write about unless it was adequately financed. So the members of the society set about buying it them-selves. Dad had never wanted to make his fortune from the zoo, all he wanted was to keep it going. This way, the debts would all be met and he'd become an employee of the society, without the fear of bailiffs and bank-ruptcy dominating every waking hour.

A price for the freehold, to include all the buildings, animals, cages and enclosures, was put at £8,216. A bank loan would have to be arranged, secured on the assets, and most of this could go to pay off the zoo's debts. A sinking fund (like a cash reserve) would then be set up which would pay for funding the loan and running the zoo. This would be financed by offering memberships. To be a 'founder' member would require a one-off payment of £500. You could become a 'benefactor' for £250. Lower down the hierarchy, 'patrons' paid an annual membership of £25 and 'life members' an annual membership of £15. Each category came with privileges – free entry for a quota of guests and use of the members' rooms. No dividends would be payable. All profits would be ploughed back into the zoo.

Reporting this in the national press, *The Times* wrote that Chester Zoo was 'not as well known as it should be, especially locally', but that, if put on a similar footing as zoos in London, Edinburgh and Bristol, it had the potential to become a national collection. 'One realises at once why zoologists all over the country take so much interest in it. For one thing there is not a hint of congestion... A kitchen garden enclosed in high brick walls has been turned into an aviary where birds may sing in the sun.'

The first objective of the new Chester Zoological Society was to 'encourage the humane treatment of wild animals and birds and assist in the preservation of wild animals and bird life in this country'.

In our own way, we were already doing that. Two fox cubs had been given to us by the local hunt after their mother had been killed. This was also to make up for the hounds killing all our white Angora rabbits – we always had rabbits because children loved them. I was at school when it happened and by the time I got back everything had been cleaned up, but Mew said it was one of the most awful sights she had ever seen. She was used to most things about animals, but this was the worst she'd ever had to deal with – a mangled mess of half-eaten bodies and bones and blood-covered fur. The hunt finally offered to pay damages and agreed that, from then on, the zoo was out of bounds under any circumstance. I think that even they had been shocked at the carnage.

Dogs in general were banned in the zoo because one day a terrier got loose and found his way to the deer pen at the edge of the orchard, where a buck fallow deer was so frightened that he died of a heart attack. There was one exception. During the war someone brought us a twelve-month-old bloodhound called Bruce, who had been bombed out of his home and had been found wandering around the streets of Birkenhead. At Mum's insistence, he joined our other evacuees. He knew he was neither a pet nor an exhibit so he appointed himself as a kind of guard dog, insisting on sleeping inside a large cage in the chimp house. When visitors tried to guess what kind of animal he was, 'dog' was never on the list.

Dad only really waged war on two wild creatures: rats and mice. The zoo's food supply would give them an easy living, he said, if they were ever allowed to breed and get out of control. We had a few cats around for this reason, but Dad later dispensed with them because he thought they brought in disease.

Cats definitely created their own problems. A family of jackdaws made their nest in a disused chimney and, when the young were learning to fly, one fell out and a kitten started playing with it. Neither Mum nor Mew could resist any creature in trouble, and Muriel was determined to keep it alive. She put it in a box and fed it, just as she would one of the tropical birds. Whereas they're generally a bit fussy, Jacky didn't care what he ate. Although he would disappear for hours, he was happiest in the kitchen, where he had made a nest on the top shelf of the dresser. And if anything shiny or colourful went missing, that's the first place we would look. Visitors took to giving him small coins, which we'd find back in his treasure trove of a 'nest'. He'd make friends with people by saying, 'Hello!', then once he'd got what he wanted, he'd fly off. He was a great chatterbox, and as good a mimic as some of the parrots, who adopted him as one of their own.

When the smaller birds were turned out into the big 'open' aviary in the kitchen garden, their old aviary against the wall became home to the parrots. We had beautiful hyacinth and blue and red macaws, rosella parrots, parakeets and lemon-crested cockatoos. The macaw called Rob Rob had his stand in the kitchen. After a day in the aviary, he'd spend the night in the house, even in the summer. It was as if once he'd finished his job – being on show to visitors – he'd go home after work. Although free to go where he pleased, Rob Rob preferred the warmth of the kitchen to anywhere else. He used to climb up the back of chairs and pop up behind you when you weren't expecting it. With me, he liked to preen the hairs on the back of my neck, lifting each one before carefully putting it back.

Birds like parrots have quite distinct personalities, and Rob Rob was a particularly nice bird and very affectionate to humans, although people who didn't know him found him a bit intimidating as he had a very large beak that he would use to take chunks of wood out of the back of chairs. But he could also be quite particular and nervous. If he didn't feel comfortable, he would show it. Once, when I was posing with Rob Rob on my shoulder for a photographer, I realised that something was wrong when he started shifting his feet. It turned out he'd messed right down the front of my frock. After a few years Dad found him a mate and so he turned his attention to her. Their romance had a happy ending as they succeeded in hatching and rearing a chick.

Winter at the zoo was always difficult. It wasn't just the cold and the damp, it was the fog, which the animals hated more than anything else. The mist would come up from the River Dee, mix with the pollution from the Birkenhead shipyards and just settle on the land, not shifting for weeks on end. While food and heating bills were higher, the number of visitors would be little more than a trickle. The animals didn't like that either. Whatever the detractors might think, they enjoyed their company, particularly the regulars, who would bring them treats. The occasions when we had what Granny called 'loutish' behaviour were very few, and the culprits would be shown the gate and banned from ever coming back.

On frosty nights all the parrots, cockatoos and macaws would come into the house for warmth. Bringing them all in was quite a job. We'd get them to hop onto a broom handle and then carry them up to the large bedroom beside my mum's, where they'd spend the night on trestle tables covered in newspaper.

Most of them were quite happy with this arrangement and didn't need much persuading. But some were really difficult. Instead of climbing on the carrying stick, they'd land on your head. Others would sit on your shoulder and so you'd have to walk back to the house and up the stairs as they were preening your hair, hoping that they didn't give your ear a nip in passing. One such, a cockatoo, hated females and I dreaded being given her as she would wander around the floor of the aviary nipping at my ankles. As for Rob Rob, he was really heavy and would inch his way along the carrying stick till I could barely hold him. I didn't dare to put him down as it would mean going through the whole business again and Rob Rob could be very contrary when he chose to be.

The ones we didn't really trust were put in cages. The rest would just roost on the tables. Rob Rob never joined the others upstairs. He considered himself far too superior. Later, after he became more interested in his mate, we had two green Amazon parrots called Laura and Lenny who would live with us at night, and on cold days they liked to sit in the ashes of the previous night's fire to keep warm. They were very close friends, practically inseparable, and would walk around the floor of the kitchen muttering away to each other. During the day they'd happily go back into the aviary. But Lily, a ring-necked parakeet, kicked up such a fuss, we gave up trying. She would just fly around the zoo during the day, visiting various animals as took her fancy. In the morning we would open the kitchen window to let her out and she would fly back in in the evening.

People sometimes imagine that birds make rather remote pets, but it's not true. Just like a dog or a cat, they enjoy being fussed over. I would spend hours when I was little just preening the feathers of the parrots and cockatoos, and they'd make it clear when they thought I'd spent long enough with one and it was now their turn. They loved being preened and preening. A few years later I remember a parakeet who would poke his beak through the mesh of the next pen and preen a fox we'd rescued.

Even the smallest finches have extra-ordinary memories and never forget a voice or a face. My mother had only to come into the courtyard and they would know immediately it was her and would flock to the corner of the aviary where they knew she would come, clamouring and calling.

I don't know what Punch was fed on in those first few months, but it could have been bran mixed with whatever Dad could get free when Chester fish market was packing up for the day and throwing out what was left over. Fish doesn't keep unless it's refrigerated, and back then there was no such thing as a cold store. He would go over twice a week to get herrings for Pelly the Pelican, who had come over from Shavington. By then he had bought a Hillman Minx – a little boxy black car – which had to do everything, including travelling to Liverpool and even as far as Portland in Dorset to pick up animals. We had it for so long that its number is imprinted on my brain: EBM 595. But whatever else it was used for, it always stank of fish.

Every autumn the local hunt would organise a point-to-point on the farmland next to Oakfield. A point-to-point is a steeplechase, a race that originally went between two churches because the spires could be seen from far away. It gave the horses an outing before the hunting season began, leaping any hedge or ditch that was in the way. It was a Saturday sometime in the autumn of 1933 and horse boxes had been arriving since early in the morning. The starting line was not a church, but directly across the road from our main gate. The first we knew that anything was wrong was when one of the farmers came up to the house. A horse had fallen at the first jump, he said, and broken its neck. When this happens there's nothing you can do except put it down, and this poor horse had had to be shot, so they were wondering if the zoo could make use of the carcass. But there was a proviso: a bit like the bears at Matlock Bath, Dad had to be able to move it. As Uncle Kit happened to be staying at the time, they both went over to take a look. It turned out to be a huge thoroughbred, a stallion, and incredibly heavy. Uncle Kit decided that, as long as there were no animals nearby to be frightened, he could butcher it on the spot. Butchering was something he knew about from slaughtering pigs on my other grandparents' farm. Once he was satisfied that no horses would be returning, he and Dad set off back to the house, fetched Mum's largest knife from the kitchen, collected some sacks and a sharpening stone and went back to the jump where the horse had fallen.

The next problem was finding somewhere to store it. Meat lasts a bit longer than fish and in fact usually needs to be hung to become tender, but even so, it needed to be kept somewhere cool. Luckily there were the extensive wine cellars under the house, which stayed at an even temperature throughout the year. Next question: who would they give it to? We only had a few carnivores at that time, a civet cat being the largest. But then Kit said, 'What about Punch?' Ever since helping to build his enclosure, he'd always had a soft spot for him.

We'd always thought of Punch as eating fish, but polar bears also eat seals so it was

117

worth a try. Uncle Kit threw a huge chunk of horseflesh down to him, he took one sniff and went absolutely mad, tearing it to pieces with his claws, gulping it down as if he had been starving, which he probably was. It was the same the next day, and the next. Punch hadn't needed a wife, he had just needed a proper diet! It was a total transformation. He took notice of everyone, began rolling over, waving his gigantic paws in the air like a giant white puppy – probably a trick remembered from his days in Bostock and Wombwell's menagerie. Within a very short time he stopped looking sad and dishevelled. He didn't even look old; he looked strong and healthy. By the time he'd eaten all the horse, Dad had discovered that horsemeat was cheap. Cheshire was a farming district and, well into the 1930s, the fields were still worked by horses pulling ploughs and harrows. Tractors were rare and expensive and didn't become common in England until after the war. What this meant was that horse-meat was readily available because – unlike in France and Belgium – it was not thought fit for human consumption.

For the zoo, it was a turning point. From then on Punch became one of the zoo's star attractions, although he still wouldn't go in the water. One thing that hadn't changed was his stubbornness.

Chapter 5

When Chester Zoological Society discussed the proposal to buy the zoo in October 1933, the only question was 'whether the society could get sufficient support to adopt it', the chairman said. Although over 31,000 people had gone through the gates that year – an average of eighty a day – and the numbers for June were up 300 per cent on 1932, without proper investment it couldn't break even, let alone build up reserves.

My father understood only too well that if the zoo didn't move forward it would slide backwards. In trying to find a solution to the problem of balancing the need to make money against his vision of a zoo without bars, he had gone to see Gerald Iles, the new go-ahead director of Belle Vue Zoo, who had taken over from his father in the spring of 1933. Gerald Iles's background couldn't have been more different from Dad's. The Iles family were originally from London and were well-off, and in 1925 an uncle had bought Belle Vue from the Jennisons, who were the original owners but who had neglected it since the war. Gerald's father was appointed to manage it, and Gerald worked alongside him, living in a flat above the main entrance.

Mr Ives, as I always knew him – and whom I considered then, aged eight, the handsomest man alive – had always been fascinated by animals. When he was a boy and living in London he would spend school holidays wandering around the Natural History Museum in Kensington or visiting Regent's Park Zoo. The family had money and, once he started working for his uncle, he visited zoos in Europe to see what was happening there, as well as taking a course in zoology at Manchester University. But the country then was deep in the Depression and industrial areas like Manchester were among the hardest hit. In 1932 the number of unemployed was 3.5 million and in some places it was as high as 70 per cent. With many families entirely dependent on the dole, they weren't likely to spend what little they had on trips to the zoo. Mr Iles Senior had become seriously ill with all the worry and retired early, leaving his son to take over.

Gerald Iles was then only twenty-one, seventeen years younger than my dad, but they became great friends because they shared the same vision about how animals should be kept. Yet Mr Iles was also a realist. He knew that to keep visitors coming back they needed to be entertained – but that didn't have to mean cheap amusements and penny arcades, it meant not being bored. Belle Vue was coming up to its hundredth anniversary and he was planning changes along similar lines to Dad's, including an open-air monkey enclosure and a gibbon mountain. He was one of my father's staunchest supporters and spoke up for him at the meeting where it was proposed that the newly founded Chester Zoological Society purchase the zoo themselves.

Another speaker, a Mr Johnson of Nantwich, said he believed everyone involved with the society wished to avoid the gardens becoming an amusement park. He came from over twenty miles away, he said, and didn't understand why the people of Chester didn't take more interest in this wonderful place on their doorstep.

The society itself was made up of so few members that it couldn't put up the money itself – they had so far only managed to raise £2,750. In the short term the remainder could be raised on the surety of the assets, but could they guarantee to be able to fund the loan? The chairman said that everyone knew that Oakfield was second to none and that it would be 'a great disaster if Chester and the county could not maintain the place as zoological gardens'.

The issue of animals v. entertainment was a problem that Bristol Zoo had been facing for years. The Bristol, Clifton and Western England Zoological Society had been set up in the nineteenth century by a wealthy section of Bristol society (including Isambard Kingdom Brunel) 'to promote the diffusion of local knowledge by facilitating observation of the habits, form and structure of the animal kingdom, as well as affording rational amusement and recreation to the visitors of the neighbourhood'. But ordinary people – the ones who came through the turnstiles – weren't that interested in scientific observation, and gradually the amusements took over from the animals. In the summer there were garden fêtes and tennis parties and boating on the lake. A roller-skating rink was made, which in the winter was flooded for ice-skating. The income coming in from the carnival and fairground activities soon outstripped takings from the gate. So it was hardly surprising that, in the 1920s, the government decided Bristol Zoo was a place of entertainment and so ineligible for tax relief as an educational facility. Inevitably this lowered the budget for its upkeep and investment in animals, and the more run-down and dowdy the zoo became, the less people wanted to go there. Then in came another young idealist called Reginald Greed, who was made director of the zoo at only twenty-three. He too shared the same vision as Mr Iles and my dad, and all three would become great friends, swapping ideas as well as animals for nearly fifty years.

The climate was definitely changing. London Zoo, originally set up by the founder of Singapore, Sir Thomas Stamford Raffles, as somewhere to house his private animal collection, was now run by the Zoological Society of London on scientific lines and was a huge success. In 1902 Dr Peter Chalmers Mitchell had been appointed as its secretary. He was a medical doctor and insisted that all the animals needed fresh air, even those used to tropical climates. This had never been done before; animals like lions and tigers had been kept in hot houses with no natural ventilation. When they got ill and died it was thought the cages weren't hot enough, that there were too many draughts, and the way things were, nobody could prove otherwise. But as soon as Dr Chalmers Mitchell moved the zoo's baboons to unheated outdoor cages, their mortality rate plummeted. He also suggested a country retreat where the animals had more space than in Regent's Park. Thirty years later, just three months before our opening day at Upton, that idea had resulted in Whipsnade, 600 acres of parkland on the edge of the Chilterns, just west of Luton.

After barely two months of trying to raise the money to buy the zoo, Chester Zoological Society accepted that they couldn't do it. There just weren't enough local residents interested, so it was decided to form a new, bigger society which brought in people living further afield, which is how the North of England Zoological Society came into being. But even that didn't go smoothly. It was the same problem – not enough people would invest.

On 1 May 1934 the *Liverpool Post* launched an appeal. The North of England Zoological Society, it said, had just four days in which to raise £350 to stop Chester Zoo closing. 'Mr G. S. Mottershead, yesterday said to the *Post*, "Already about £5,000 has been subscribed by interested persons. The sum further required is not much, if only other friends of the zoo will realise the urgency... Any person desiring to help may do so by donating a sum of money to the funds, for which he or she will receive certain privileges; or they may loan any amount in denominations of £25 which will be secured up to the amount actually required."' It even reached the national press – the headline in the *Daily Express* read: NEW ZOO'S RACE WITH TIME.

Who that final £350 came from, I don't know, or whether it was one donation or several, or came in as a loan. But by 16 May the *Manchester Guardian* had confirmed that the North of England Zoological Society had been registered at Somerset House, the directors, for the purposes of registration, being Mr George Mottershead of Upton-by-Chester; Mr Gerald Iles of Belle Vue Zoo, Manchester; and Miss Geraldine Russell Allen of Davenham Hall, Northwich. The newspaper wished the zoo well. 'It is hoped that the coming season will draw still more visitors and that the North of England Zoological Society will thrive.'

The society took over management of Chester Zoo on 13 June 1934, overseen by an elected council of twenty-one members. George Mottershead was appointed director secretary at £3 a week. The catering manager was Elizabeth Mottershead at £1 a week and the assistant curator was Muriel Mottershead at 10/- a week. The family's lodgings and food would be paid for by the society. Gardeners and other staff were 'to be employed and controlled by the director secretary within the limits of the cash at his disposal'. Which, when everything else was accounted for, amounted to £13.

This new financial security meant that Dad could finally get someone in to help Granddad. He was now seventy-eight years old and could no longer do the heavy work. I can still remember the day when Charlie Collins arrived. As assistant gardener he was paid 7/- a week plus his keep and he slept in the servants' quarters on the first floor, the other side of the back stairs that we all now used because the main staircase was closed off. I don't know if Charlie had any gardening experience, but in fact he didn't need any. He was young, strong, hard-working and willing, and that was good enough for Granddad. The apprenticeship he would get would be second to none.

I had just had my eighth birthday. Charlie was sixteen, not much more than a boy himself, and I adored him. He would put me in the wheelbarrow and career across the lawn until I was helpless with laughter and then he'd tip me out while Mary would be crowing and turning cartwheels on the lawn until it was her turn. He was like the elder brother I never had and we remained friends right up until his death.

Charlie had been brought up in the National Children's Home in Frodsham, a village outside Runcorn, about ten miles to the east. He had never known his mother; he always supposed she'd been made to give him up because he was illegitimate. He'd been born a cockney and to this day I have no idea how he ended up in Cheshire, and neither did he. According to the Salvation Army, which was all he had to go on, he had been taken from his mum at birth.

Not long after Charlie's arrival, three other boys joined the staff. They were called Sam, Billy and Nippy, who was Welsh, and all four boys slept together in one room. In fact they had the best of it, being directly over the kitchen. Charlie used to tell me how shocked he was when he first arrived at how cold the house was. He'd always imagined that a mansion like Oakfield would have central heating, but he said it was colder than the dormitories at Frodsham. In fact it did have central heating – there were big cast-iron radiators in all the main rooms, including the bedrooms – but it was never used as we couldn't afford to light the boiler. Whereas most people, when they got into bed, would get undressed, I would put more clothes on, even though I had filled a hot-water bottle made of stone.

Although officially Sam, Billy and Nippy were down as trainee keepers, they had to turn their hands to anything Dad wanted them to do. Nobody who worked for Mr Mott, as everyone called him, ever had only one job, and with Nippy being very tall, Dad chose him as the zoo's walking advertisement. He had a sandwich board made to fit, and whenever there was an event within ten miles – like a village fête or a whist drive – Dad would deliver Nippy there in the car and drop him off. He'd then have to walk around until Dad came back to pick him up a few hours later. Dad wasn't averse to doing the publicity himself, however. One year, during the Frodsham village carnival, he filled the car with branches of laurel and in the passenger seat jammed the stuffed bear head that usually hung on the wall in the hall. It really did look like a wild bear peering out of the undergrowth. He joined the back of the floats, and in the back window of the car placed a big card saying 'Visit Chester Zoo'.

When it came to promotion, Dad was tireless. He put together a film show about the zoo and the animals and would take it round to village halls, giving talks, and I would sometimes go with him as his assistant. One time I remember the film not rewinding on the spool, and when the lights came on afterwards, a little boy sitting next to him was covered with unravelled film. Once Dad was invited to give a talk at a 13th-century manor house called Northop Hall outside a village also called Northop Hall, but instead he went to the village hall. He found it odd that the audience seemed so restless and didn't seem to know what he was on about. It wasn't until the person who was supposed to be giving the talk turned up that his mistake was realised and Dad hurried off to the other one.

He never missed a trick. He took me to the launch of the latest Cunard liner, the new *Mauretania*, in July 1938, which was then the largest ship ever to have been built in England. It was at the Cammell Laird shipyard in Birkenhead, and was a great occasion. I had never seen crowds like it – 50,000

128

people were there to watch her sliding down the slipway into the Mersey. Nippy came along too, with his sandwich board, not for the fun of it, like me, nor even to advertise it to local people – Birkenhead was only seventeen miles away from Upton – but on the off-chance that it would be filmed by Pathé News and be seen in cinemas around the country.

Although Charlie Collins was the zoo's first properly paid member of staff, Dad had had unpaid help in the shape of another Charlie, Granddad's youngest son, the brother who had been too young to fight in the war. Now, like millions of other working-class men, Uncle Charlie had lost his job, which had also meant losing his home. Perhaps Mum and Dad were warned that they were coming – I don't know – but in my memory they turned up out of the blue: Uncle Charlie, Auntie Jessie and my three cousins, Stanley, who was about twelve, Patricia, known as Paddy, aged nine, and George, seven, a few months older than me. They stayed for eighteen months, only leaving when my uncle found another job.

They didn't stay in the big house with us because it was by then too full, with the boys and Dad's office, not to mention the parrots. Instead they stayed at the lodge with Granddad and Granny. It can't have been easy being all crammed in together like that. Although there were three bedrooms, it didn't have electricity – the lamps were gas and you'd have to put pennies in the meter. There was no indoor lavatory, just a privy at the bottom of the garden.

My two youngest cousins went to the village school and, as far as I know, they experienced no trouble, but perhaps they'd been warned not to make a big thing of living at the zoo, though they had the same surname as us so it should have been obvious. Stan went to the City Grammar School in Chester and he would come to the convent to meet me and put me on the bus back to Upton. Like me when I got older, he would cycle in and out of Chester, and on the way home he'd go via Dean's bakery, to pick up the stale loaves which they would give us for nothing. They'd put them in a sack and he'd have to push his bike all the way back to the zoo, balancing the sack over the crossbar.

George was the closest to me in age and also the only one interested in animals so he would regularly come over to play. I taught him not to be frightened of Pelly, our pelican. Pelly had been at the zoo longer than anyone except Adam and Eve and so he considered himself one of the family. Although he had his own pen, it didn't stop him getting out. If we weren't on time with his herrings he'd flap over his fence, waddle to the scullery and demand his tea. He was happy to stay where he was supposed to as long as his schedule was adhered to. Paddy rarely went further from the lodge than the pay box, where Auntie Jessie had taken over from Granny. The few times she did come over to the house, she'd just fiddle with the typewriter in the office.

No sooner did one crisis fade, than another appeared. In 1934 a parcel of farmland next to Oakfield was put up for sale with planning permission for a housing development. The society agreed it would be a disaster if houses were built right up against the boundary. An urgent meeting of the council was called and somehow the money was raised. It had always been understood that the zoo had to expand. That was one reason my father had been convinced that Oakfield was the right location for it. It was surrounded by farmland which, when the zoo was making money, could be bought. The existing gardens were an important part of the zoo's appeal and so couldn't be touched. It was the same with the orchard – Dad had plans to turn it into a wild bird sanctuary and the apples and pears were an important source of food for the animals. He was already thinking of the zoo's long-term development, which in his mind included big cats, and they would need to have space. Nine acres may sound a lot, but it wasn't. If the zoo was to have a future, it had to be able to grow. We couldn't afford to buy all of the land up for sale, but we bought twenty-three acres of it. A Mr Martin bought the rest – seventeen acres – as a riding school. (The zoo eventually acquired that too, in 1958.)

So now, for the first time, Dad was able to put his idea of an enclosure surrounded by a ditch rather than bars into practice. It would be based on the principles of the German Carl Hagenbeck. Hagenbeck's father – originally a fishmonger in Hamburg – had begun to import wild animals in the nineteenth century, starting with some seals that the skipper of a trawler had brought him by mistake. As zoos became increasingly fashionable across Europe and America – both private collections and ambitious large city zoos – the demand for exotic animals became even greater, and Hagenbeck was soon making a fortune importing them to Germany and then transporting them to wherever they were wanted. He became the most successful animal trader in the world – at one point he was said to have twenty elephants in stock. Parallel to this, he started training big cats, again with great success, ending up with a lion-taming act that he toured across Europe. From there he moved on to breeding and decided he needed the facilities of a zoo with plenty of land for expansion.

'I desired above all things', he wrote in his

autobiography, 'to give the animals the maximum of liberty... I wished to exhibit them not as captives, confined within narrow spaces, and looked at between bars but as free to wander from place to place within as large limits as possible.'

Since the eighteenth century English landscape gardeners had constructed ditches, known as ha-has, which separated formal lawns around the house from the countryside beyond. These ditches prevented cows and horses that grazed the parkland from getting too close to the house, while maintaining the impression of a pastoral scene with an uninterrupted view. It had started with deer parks in England in the Middle Ages; ditches with one vertical wall allowed deer to enter a nobleman's land but not to leave, which was how they built up their herds of what were wild animals. As long as one side was steep enough, the deer couldn't get out. As a solution for a zoo, it had the added advantage of being cheap. Once the original ditch or moat was dug, there would be no further costs. No metalwork or iron mesh to rust or rot and nothing that would need painting or replacing. The only thing it required – which most zoos didn't have – was space.

Based on all the knowledge he had gained from training animals, Carl Hagenbeck knew that each species had a maximum leap, both vertically and horizontally. To keep visitors safe, a lion would need a different width of ditch from a tiger or a bear, and it was important to know this; it would literally be the difference between life and death. He also designed the enclosures so an animal would never get an open approach, to prevent it building up speed and making a running jump. He started construction of his zoo in a suburb outside Hamburg in 1902, the same year that my father, aged eight, went to Belle Vue and decided he would make a 'zoo without bars'.

The *tiergarten* at Stellingen opened in 1907 and was an immediate success. Wild animals appeared to be mingling with each other, species that would never have been safe if they'd really been together. Visitors weren't aware of the ditches or moats because they were disguised by planting. The zoo in Stellingen would become the blueprint for the zoos of the future, including Chester.

The first enclosure built along these lines at Upton was for the Malayan bears, and my father started planning it the moment Sally arrived. She was presented to the zoo by her owner, Mr Eaton Parker, who'd had her as a pet, but who'd decided she had become too boisterous. However, he assured Dad that she was very gentle and affectionate and used to people. Malayan sun bears are the smallest of all the bears and rarely grow over five feet in height.

The weather was cold the day Sally arrived and with nowhere arranged for her first night, we put her in one of the spare rooms in the attic, which was completely empty except for some metal boxes of Dad's filled with papers and old photographs. Anything else, Mew said, would have been cruel as she was used to sleeping in her owner's house. When Oakfield had first been built, this room had been the nursery so the windows were barred and there was just linoleum on the floor. But the next morning, when Mew went in to see if she was all right, she found nothing except a mass of torn newspaper. As it was still early she didn't want to raise the alarm without first searching herself.

Mew and I were sharing a bedroom by then and I woke up to find my sister whispering in my ear and trying not to laugh.

'Get up, lazy bones, and come with me. I've got something to show you!'

We crept out of our bedroom and stopped outside Dad's bedroom door. 'But, Mew, you can't go in there,' I protested.

'Yes, I can. He's away, don't you remember?'

So in we went, and there, under the eiderdown, was Sally, fast asleep. As for Dad's bed, it was completely soaked. She had found a cold hot-water bottle he had left there and chewed the end off.

Back in the thirties, keeping exotic animals

135

as pets was quite common, particularly among the upper classes who travelled a lot and thus had easy access to animals and plenty of servants to care for them. They treated these pets a bit like they treated their children – handed them over to the ayah when they got bored. It was harder to do that in England than it was in Malaya or Kenya or Ceylon, and by the thirties the British Empire was coming to an end – it had already been renamed the British Commonwealth – and many of our colonies were already on the way to independence. People who until then had lived a life of ease in the tropics were finding out that things weren't so simple back in England. Also it was one thing keeping a pet animal in the country where it was born: food wouldn't be a problem, nor the climate, nor illness. It was quite different in a country which was damp and cold and where tropical fruit was hard to obtain and expensive. And when an animal grew too big or became a nuisance in some other way, it could be easily got rid of in the country of its birth, but in England it was a different matter, as only the wealthy could keep staff to look after their pets, which was why so many ended up with us.

There are plenty of people even today who treat their dogs in a similar fashion, but instead of being an Afghan or a shih-tzu, back then it was a monkey, or in the case of

Sally, a bear. But dogs have been domesticated by man and are no longer wild creatures. Bears and monkeys are different.

I remember one terrible time when the Hon. Mrs Arthur Baillie arrived one afternoon and handed over a Humboldt's woolly monkey. She didn't live locally, but had driven all the way from Banbury, south of Birmingham, because she'd heard that Dad never turned an animal away and would give Monk a good home. Mew asked me to have a look at him and see what I thought. Woolly monkeys are very endearing and cuddly, and to see him standing on the floor of the pen whimpering was heartbreaking. He was quite large, with thick grey hair, and while I was watching, he put his head in his hands and began to sob. There's no other word for it. There may not have been tears, but this poor monkey was in real distress.

'Poor little fellow, he's homesick,' Mew said. 'He's probably been mollycoddled all his life, and now this – just abandoned.'

'Perhaps Mum will know what to do,' I suggested.

Mew sighed. 'Well, there's no harm in trying, though I've probably had more experience with monkeys than she has. While you're there, cut up an apple and bring it back, will you?'

I went back to the kitchen and was just telling Mum when we heard the car pull up outside and a few minutes later Dad walked in. 'Couldn't we just bring him into the house?' I asked him. 'He's a pet.'

'Yes, but not your pet, June, or Mew's pet. He's not a baby who is happy to go with anyone. He wants his own family, not us.'

'You mean Mrs Baillie.'

'Yes.'

'But Mrs Baillie lives miles away.'

He said nothing.

'Please Dad. Just for one night?'

'No,' he said. 'That would only make it worse. He has to sink or swim.' He wasn't going to get involved, he said. 'Mew must deal with this on her own.'

I don't know how she managed not to take him out of the cage and cuddle him. My sister's instinct to comfort a distressed animal was very strong. But she didn't. Instead she had a brain-wave. Other animals' distress can communicate itself and be a problem, but she knew that Mary, in particular, was good at recognising it and being a comfort. So Monk was put in a cage in the chimp house beside her. It took a few days for him to calm down, but eventually he did. As for Mrs Baillie, she never came to visit him, and perhaps that was a good thing.

The new land proved ideal as a bear enclosure. It already had a large cowshed, part of which could serve as a den, providing warmth, shelter and privacy. There was also an ancient oak tree, many hundreds of years old, Dad said, that he decided would be perfect for them to climb. And as it was grassland, they could forage, dig holes, do whatever they would do in the wild. The ditch would be circular, with the tree at its centre, allowing visitors to watch them from every direction. Most important of all, there would be no bars.

Until her permanent home was ready, Sally took up residence in one of the former loose boxes around the courtyard. That's how it always happened; animals would be moved around and found temporary quarters. Some would have to share with others and it was sometimes surprising who got on with whom. There was an ibis and a rabbit, I remember, who became inseparable.

Another new resident was Charlie the jackass penguin. He was housed with Minnie the tapir and shared her pool. He hadn't come from Antarctica, but from warmer waters off the coast of South Africa. Originally he'd had a wife, but she'd died within two weeks of arriving. Penguins are monogamous and it was clear that he was pining – his wailing was pitiful. Dad warned me that he was probably going to die too, and that I should prepare for the worst. But a few weeks later a visitor from the north of England came, saw Charlie on his own, recognised what was wrong and offered to present the zoo with her pet penguin as a companion, although she didn't know if hers was a girl or a boy. All Dad had to do was to collect it from the other side of Preston. It turned out to be a girl and I christened her Sadie.

Charlie perked up the moment she arrived. The problem was that Sadie showed no interest in him. Worse than that, she went out of her way to avoid him. She refused to go in the pool when he was in it. She refused to eat when he was having his herrings. She made it clear to everyone – if not to him - that she intended to have nothing to do with this forced marriage. To avoid his attentions, she took to the water and only came out when herrings were on offer.

So then Charlie tried another tack – building a nest – piling stone upon stone, their purpose being to stop eggs rolling about once they'd been laid. Then he sat on it for days, hoping that Sadie would get the idea. Penguins share incubation duties in the wild, in order that each one can hunt for their own food, so it was all perfectly natural. She took no notice. Finally he pinned her into the corner of the pen and a few days later we saw there were two eggs. From then on Charlie did nothing but fuss over her, anxiously awaiting his turn at sitting on them. Eventually two chicks emerged, none the worse for wear. Charlie and Sadie fed the babies beak-to-beak for about five months – regurgitating herrings that they'd been fed by hand. But then, while the babies were still too young to feed themselves, Sadie laid two more eggs. It was too much. She couldn't cope with feeding them as well as sitting on the new eggs and one morning, when I came down to look in on them before I went to school, I found her floating face down in her pool. The babies were already dead. Although I was by now used to seeing dead animals, I cried. Penguin chicks are among the most endearing tiny creatures you can imagine, all white fluff and beak.

It's difficult not to get anthropomorphic at times like this and I can only say that, to me, Charlie appeared distraught. At night he would start his wailing again, and during the day he would build nests and sit on the stones, hoping, I suppose, that they would hatch. Again Dad told me to expect the worst.

'Why don't you just buy another penguin?' I asked.

'We can't afford it,' he said.

'You can have what's in my money box,' I said. I had a porcelain pig with a hole in his back that I would drop coins into when I got them. I would take them out occasionally, using a knife, to buy sweets.

'That's very generous of you, June, but I don't think you'd have enough.'

141

'But I've got nearly ten shillings!'

'A female penguin would cost £10.'

Eventually somebody decided that all that Charlie needed was company and a rabbit was put in his enclosure, and they soon became friends, or at least companions. When the rabbit was given carrots, Charlie would steal them for his latest nest. Then, when Charlie wasn't looking, the rabbit would take them back again. That was all during the day, but at night he would remember Sadie and his lost chicks and I would hear him wailing.

The original pair of penguins had been given by Miss Doris Russell Allen. There were three Russell Allen sisters – the other two were Miss Geraldine and Miss Diana – and they all lived at Davenham Hall, near Northwich. They were all animal mad – Miss Diana once gave me a book she'd written about her pure white Chihuahua – though Miss Geraldine was the one I got to know best because she was a member of the council and would regularly appear at the council meetings. She became one of the zoo's major benefactors, and it was her money that was building the aquarium that the council had decided would be the first venture after they took over.

Miss Geraldine was the oldest of the sisters, born in 1893, and very rich. In 1905 their father had inherited the *Manchester Evening News* from his uncle. In 1924 it was sold to the *Manchester Guardian*. They were the equivalent then of multi-millionaires.

She was a few years younger than my mum and had been twenty-one when the war broke out. I never knew if there was a sad love story, if she'd had a sweetheart who had died in the trenches, but young officers were as likely to be killed as privates, if not more so – her brother John never came back. When I got to know her, she was about forty – which seemed older then than it does now – and no more suitors would be asking for her hand in marriage, however rich she was. She was still a 'Miss' when she passed away in 1976, as were both her sisters.

Because of the war, there was a whole generation of women who never had the chance to marry and have children, and in my view it was no coincidence that so many of the zoo's benefactors were unmarried. The energy and emotions that they would otherwise have devoted to their families had to have an outlet, and that outlet was often animals. Miss Geraldine was no different. It was said she had twenty dogs and even had a special groom whose only job was to look after them.

Ever since I'd fallen in love with the white Pekinese that boarded in the kennels at Shavington, I'd longed for a dog. Dad was always saying, 'One day, one day,' and I think he'd always intended to get me one. It was all

143

right thinking the animals were my friends, but he didn't want me getting too close. When Babs had arrived from Shavington she had been sicker than anyone realised. It turned out to be TB, and in those days there was nothing you could do. Although Muriel did her best, Babs didn't last long. TB is very infectious, but I was too young to understand why I couldn't go and see her. I had been heartbroken. I think Dad thought that if I had a dog, I could lavish it with all my affection without the risk of being hurt.

One morning Miss Russell Allen arrived at the house with two smooth-haired Lilliputian terrier puppies, one under each arm. Miss Russell Allen was very grand. She always arrived in a chauffeur-driven car and had the most beautiful clothes. Her hats were decorated with bits of fur or feathers and she never wore the same outfit twice and always smelled lovely. When you stood close to her, it was like being inside Granddad's hot house.

She breezed in like she always did, but instead of going off with Dad, she called me over.

'What do you think, dear? Aren't they adorable?'

'Yes,' I said. They looked sweet.

'Your father tells me you've just had a birthday, so I thought, as they're little and you're little, you might get along.'

I looked at my dad. Had I heard right? Was she giving them to me?

'What's this, June, lost your tongue? Doesn't Miss Russell Allen even deserve a thank you?'

'Thank you, Miss Russell Allen,' I said.

'Now, off with you to the kitchen,' my dad said, 'and introduce your new charges to Mew and your mother before I change my mind,' and he gave me one of his winks as he ushered his visitor into the library.

She was right, the puppies were adorable. One had a white body with a black face and the other was black all over. I called them Trixie and Jet, thinking one was a girl and one was a boy. In fact both of them were girls, but by the time I found that out they already had their names. Although they were from the same litter, they weren't identical twins, and Jet was much friendlier, so when Dad said that he thought that two puppies were a bit much, I wasn't that upset when Trixie went back to Miss Russell Allen.

Jet never went on a lead, she didn't need to. She knew her name and would come if I called. Most of the time she just followed me around. We did all the usual things – I'd throw her a stick or a ball and she'd scamper off to bring it back, and she never got tired. The fact that we were in a zoo made no difference – we just had more space to play in and she didn't have to learn how to cross a main road.

Jet became my constant companion and when Mum got me a small second-hand bicycle, Jet and I would go racing around the grounds, weaving in and out of the shrubberies, down the drive to visit Granny, along the rows of apple trees in the orchard. Although she was tiny, Jet could run faster than I could pedal and would sometimes stop in her tracks and turn back her head as if to say, 'Well? What's keeping you, slow-coach?'

One morning Dad said he had a board meeting and that I had to keep quiet and not talk to anyone because important people were coming. So when Miss Russell Allen arrived, I said nothing.

'Aren't you going to say hello, dear?'

I looked at her, then lowered my eyes.

'Are you all right?'

I nodded.

'And Jet, nothing wrong with her, I trust?'

I shook my head.

'So whatever can be the matter, child?'

I moved closer and, as quietly as I could, whispered, 'Are you important?'

'Not remotely.'

'Oh good,' I said, smiling up at her.

'Why do you ask?'

'Because if you were, I've been told not to talk to you today.' Although she didn't laugh at the time – she was much too well-bred for that – she found it highly amusing and, of course, told my father, and so it became one of those family stories that stick with you all your life.

Once Uncle Charlie, Auntie Jessie and my cousins had gone back to Didsbury, I began to spend more time with my grandfather. And now that he had Charlie Collins to do the heavy work, he could spend more time in the walled garden where he grew his auriculas as well as all the vegetables. The café now offered a menu of cold lunches, and Granddad grew the salads. Cucumbers were grown in a special cold frame, like a sandpit, which had a glass roof which slid back when it was sunny. There were beans climbing on poles, lashed together like Indian tepees, and peas twining their way skywards on hazel twigs that he would get me to collect from hedges in the lane. Radishes came up in neat rows, the seeds planted at weekly intervals, and every day he let me pull some out for the café. When you went in the greenhouse, the smell of the tomatoes was something wonderful, much better than the taste. He told me that where he'd served his apprenticeship in Didsbury, tomatoes were grown for show, not to eat, and that the pineapples had very sharp thorns on their leaves.

Although Granddad was very imposing – much taller than my father, even when he stooped – I never once heard him raise his voice and he always had time to answer my questions, however simple they must have seemed. When children saw him working in the garden, they would think that he was Father Christmas, because that's who he looked like – all white beard and bushy eyebrows. Like Granny, he always wore a hat – in his case, a cap, except on special occasions when he wore a Homburg – and his one vice, as he used to call it, was a pipe, which dangled from his mouth even when it wasn't lit.

I would escape to the kitchen garden whenever I could. Jet would rush around, poking her nose under the greenhouses and potting shed, sniffing out rats, while Granddad would get me to do some weeding, looking for groundsel and dandelions, which I would then give to the rabbits as a treat. Or, if he was digging, I'd collect worms that he turned up and put them in a jam jar to give to the toads in the conservatory. I would do anything to get out of working in the Oakfield café. We had two girls, Enid and Ruby, who were only about fourteen and straight out of school. Like the boys, they lived in, in the rooms that used to be the nursery. Their job was to work in the café and care for the rest us, doing the washing and ironing and generally helping Mum out.

When I think of the café now, I think of those endless stacks of dirty dishes waiting to be washed up at the end of the day. (The only dishwasher we had was a human one, often me.) I think of emptying the teapots of their tea leaves (which Granddad liked me to keep for his roses) and swilling them out, and filling the salt and peppers and buttering the bread. I detested it all.

The salads for lunch had to be got ready every morning before the gate opened. We washed and prepared them in the butler's pantry where the plates were kept in huge stacks that were always threatening to topple over. Each salad consisted of two lettuce leaves, a tomato, a few slices of cucumber and some radishes. To go with it, there was either tinned red salmon or a slice of boiled ham. When you'd taken the order, all you had to do was add the fish or meat to the salad, which had already been arranged on the plate. When I got older, I'd help out with the waitressing, but that was nearly as bad. Never having mixed much with ordinary people, I was shy of strangers and terrified that I'd forget what they'd ordered. Not that there was that much choice: tea, either a pot for one or a pot for two, salad with salmon or ham, or sandwiches. The van from Dean's bakery would arrive early in the morning, and we had a big machine to cut the bread, because pre-sliced didn't exist back then. The next job would be to butter it. We'd make the butter soft by leaving it overnight beside the range. Like with the salads, all you had to do when you got the order for the sandwiches was to put in the filling, cheese or ham.

Another of my jobs was standing at the counter in the main hall, minding the till for the café. This I didn't mind doing, as all I had to do was wait for the customers to come and pay for their teas or their food. There was also a display case with guides, postcards, sweets, chocolates, cigarettes and matches, which I enjoyed arranging creatively to catch the customers' attention. Whenever the weather was sunny, and especially on bank holidays, the café was always busy, and when the members had their meetings sometimes they'd give me tips. Once I was given a ten shilling note from Mr Holt for 'working hard'. He said he'd heard I'd been helping Mew with a sick chimp. Mew was furious – that was all she earned in a week! But in the odd moments of quiet when no one was waiting to pay, and having rearranged the guidebooks and post-cards to my satisfaction, I would gaze around at the stuffed heads of animals shot by big-game hunters in the last century – a water buffalo, antelope and Himalayan bear – who looked down on me balefully with their glass eyes, and I had to pinch myself that this was the same room I had sat in that first night with the lovebirds, freezing cold and with only candles for lighting.

Chapter 6

With no structural work involved, the aquarium – the first project to be given the go-ahead once the new council was in place – was soon ready and the grand opening was on Wednesday 3 September 1934.

Dad had been drawing up the plans since the first time he saw the house. The idea was really simple. In the basement was a labyrinth of wine cellars, and set into the walls – the foundations really – were deep shelves where cases of wine would have been stored in their hundreds. All that was needed was for tanks of reinforced concrete, fronted by reinforced plate glass, to be built to fit the spaces. The first stage, which took up just one of the cellars, was six cold-water tanks. And once they were completed, the aquarium just grew and grew, one tank after another, whenever there was any spare time to work on it. By the time the war started all four 'rooms' in the cellar were completely full, twenty-six tanks in all, the size depending on the space, but some of them hundreds of cubic feet of water.

The aquarium was opened by Lady Daresbury, one of the founder members of the Chester Zoological Society. Her husband, Baron Daresbury of Walton, was a brewery millionaire (Greenall Whitley) and died a few years later, but his widow continued to be involved with the zoo until her death in 1953. My job that evening was to present her with a basket of flowers which concealed a tin containing tiny tropical fish. Not a neat plastic container or a Thermos, but an ordinary tin can that had once contained red salmon, wrapped round with newspaper and covered by a woollen cloth to conserve the heat.

Compared with what was to come, those first six tanks were a disappointment, at least to me. I had seen tropical fish in the aquarium at Belle Vue Zoo, when I had gone with Dad to visit Mr Iles, and they were beautiful – it was a magical world of creatures I had never known existed. And not only fish, but seahorses and sea urchins and waving fronds of underwater plants. Ever since that visit, a few months before, I'd imagined ours was going to be like that. But at the beginning the most colourful fish we had were the shubunkins, which are basically a kind of goldfish with more deeply forked tails and splashes of red.

The farmland round where we were was mainly clay, which meant there were ponds everywhere. It was from these that Granddad had caught the rudd he put in the concrete pools in the garden. This time Billy and Sam were sent out to set traps to get more. Perch and golden tench had been donated by someone who lived a few miles away in Flint in north Wales. Although they were all native fish, lit up in the aquarium they looked beautiful: perch with their striped backs, and roach with their red or golden fins. Watching a fish swimming in clear water is quite different to seeing it in a murky pond or, worse, on a fishmonger's slab.

By the end of the year there were six more tanks, this time heated and for freshwater tropical fish, many of them from the vast rivers and lakes of South and Central America. One of the first was over six feet wide and contained angelfish, black mollies, red swordtails and blue gouramis.

By then we had over fifty species of fish, as well as axolotls, the Mexican walking fish, which has legs and is not actually a fish at all but an amphibian, a kind of salamander. Later, when we had more tanks, we decided to put different species in separate tanks, so people could identify them more easily than when they were all mixed in together. It also resolved the problem of carnivorous species preying on smaller fry, though it didn't stop the problem of them eating their own eggs.

The aquarium had already proved incredibly popular. Of course it was useful to have somewhere dry to go when it rained or was cold, but there was something mesmerising about watching the glimmering fish in their illuminated tanks, carrying on their business unaware of the eyes following every swish of their tails. Visitors would stay down there for ages, because the fish were always busy doing something, often related to breeding.

We fed them on Bemax, like wheatgerm, which Mum would sprinkle on my porridge in the mornings and add to stews to thicken them up. One of my jobs was to collect daphnia from the local ponds – around Upton they were known as water fleas. Carnivorous species got scraped horsemeat or finely chopped horses' hearts, depending on their size. You can't be squeamish if you work in a zoo, and nothing is ever wasted, or wasn't in our day. After the point-to-point where the horse broke his neck, his head was given to our pair of Griffon vultures, and they loved it, and that's what they had from then on. Not that visitors ever realised. Dad said it didn't need to be broadcast, as they wouldn't appreciate it, and he was probably right. Unlike other birds of prey, vultures only ever eat carrion, so live animals were quite safe. One day a kitten found its way up onto the nesting platform and I noticed it creeping along, intent on stealing some of the vultures' food. I was convinced it was done for, but they barely gave it a passing glance.

In January 1935 one of Dad's and my dreams came true when Miss Russell Allen, helped by another member, presented the zoo with its first lion cubs. They were orphans – as were most lions who came to us in the early days – so Mew reared them by hand. My sister was wonderful with young animals of any kind. They needed gentleness and patience, both of which she had in abundance, far more so than me. Baby animals are not necessarily cuddly – I remember a porcupine she hand-reared, a large African one. It developed such a strong bond with her that even when it was fully grown it used to sit on her knee, with all its quills sticking out to prevent anyone else muscling in.

It was bitterly cold the winter when the lion cubs arrived, so until the weather warmed up they lived with us in the house. They were like great big kittens, full of fun and energy, wanting to play when they were awake, though they also spent a lot of time sleeping in a big cardboard box filled with an old blanket. As there were two of them, Mew would allow me to cuddle one while she bottle-fed the other. They grew very quickly and were constantly under our feet – prowling around, looking for things to eat or someone or something to play with. Like house cats, they liked nothing better than to sharpen their claws on the furniture, though the damage was of a rather different order and all too soon Dad said they had to get used to a pen. Perhaps it was too early to put them outside, or there was another cold snap, because it wasn't long before they died. The next two lion orphans arrived from a Nigerian chief who'd given them to the Holt family. Miss Holt passed them on to us, and the whole cycle started up again. These two lionesses did survive and were eventually exchanged with Dublin Zoo for an adult male called Patrick, who would go on to father a large family. He was a sweet-tempered lion and would let cubs – and not only his – to take liberties with him when they played, which no other lion would have allowed.

Dad was determined to build up a strong collection of lions. Although in the early days quite a few died, mainly through illness, the breeding programme was eventually so successful that lion cubs and lionesses were always on the exchange list. I've forgotten the names of most of them now, but some will remain with me all my life, either because I became attached to them, or because there were other reasons for me to remember, and not always happy ones.

Plans for the lion enclosure – designed, like the bear enclosure, on the Hagenbeck principle of a ditch and plenty of space to roam around – were already well underway, and by February 1937 a scale model of four feet to one inch was on view in the entrance hall. Nothing like it had been seen in England before and there was a great deal of controversy.

The zoo now had the space; Oakfield's original nine acres had risen to thirty-two. The lion enclosure would extend to an acre, making it the largest in Britain. The ditch would end in a high terrace from where visitors could watch in complete safety; just as if they were in a treehouse in Africa. The arches supporting the terrace would house another café and a buffet. The field itself had plenty of mature trees, which would not only give a natural look, but provide the lions with plenty of shade. Above all there would be no bars.

But, of course, Dad was faced with the usual problem. It wasn't just the cost of materials – to build something of this scope, they would need to bring in outside labour. Until now, everything had been built by Dad, Uncle Charlie, Uncle Kit and Charlie Collins. A lady member of the council had offered to match any money raised for the lion enclosure, on condition that it was up and running by July 1938, to take advantage of the summer visitors. The additional amount needed was put at £550. But the council weren't convinced it could be raised in the time – a little over a year – and didn't feel able to underwrite it. A suggestion was made that the plans be modified to reduce the cost. At thirty feet in width, the ditch took up considerably more space than bars, and those dimensions couldn't change, Dad explained. An alternative was to have a twelve-foot-high fence with a three-foot inward overhang. It would be perfectly safe, he said, and the lions would have the same amount of space: enough so that the grass didn't get worn away, enough for them to roam around and play. If the total area was reduced, he said, it would result in a much smaller enclosure, which would entirely defeat the object.

'Lions are not squirrels,' he said. 'They can't climb twelve-foot-high fences.'

Initially the council was sceptical and half of them threatened to resign. But Dad was insistent. There would be no bars. So a compromise was reached, and the foundation stone for the new enclosure was laid by Viscount Leverhulme in October 1937.

The lion house, which the outdoor enclosure would be part of, was by this time already built – mainly by Charlie. Dad had done his usual thing of showing him what to do and then leaving him to it. There were two distinct sections. In the first, the lions would be on show to the public, but the second was a den, where Dad hoped cubs would be born in privacy. He already had three mature lionesses – Faith, Hope and

Charity – who had come from Bristol Zoo in exchange for two mandrills. All he needed now was a male.

Until the lions took over in the public's affections, Punch was perhaps our biggest star – he was certainly the most photographed – but he wasn't easy.

'Why is Punch's pen so dirty?' Dad said one day to Mew.

'Because Billy can't get in to clean it, Dad. It isn't his fault. You know what Punch is like. Stubborn isn't the word. In fact, come to think of it, he reminds me of someone else...' But Dad hadn't heard her; he'd gone off in search of Billy.

'But I promise you, Mr Mott, I really have tried. He just won't go in his den, and you've always said not to trust him.'

'Well, some important people are coming tomorrow, so everything has to be shipshape, and frankly this just isn't good enough. I suppose I'll have to do it myself.'

As Punch had chosen to go to sleep against the gate, Dad took off his jacket, lowered a ladder into a corner and quietly began to climb down. When he got to the bottom, he reached up and Billy passed him a broom. He then crossed to the tap, turned the hose on and began sluicing the floor. Meanwhile Punch was sleeping, oblivious to everything. Or so it seemed. But suddenly, without any warning, he sprang into life, gave a warning growl and bounded across to where Dad was working.

'Watch out!' Billy yelled, but Dad had already made a dash for the ladder, flinging down the brush as he went. He had nearly reached safety when Punch snatched at his leg and got hold of a shoe. The ladder wobbled, but Billy was holding it firm, and Dad grabbed at his hand.

'Pull, for God's sake pull!' Dad yelled.

'I don't want to dislocate your arms, Mr Mott!'

'Forget my bloody arms, boy! Just pull!'

So Billy heaved, but still Punch had Dad's shoe in his jaw and was shaking it back and forth. Punch must have bitten through the laces, because suddenly Dad was free, but the shoe was still hanging out of Punch's jaw.

Keepers had to be able to deal with any animal or bird in the zoo, and Dad was always very clear about bears. It didn't matter how sweet and cuddly they looked, they were totally untrustworthy, he said, the most untrustworthy animals in any zoo, and a polar bear was the most dangerous one of all. A few weeks earlier a peacock had flown onto the wall of the pen, and Punch had grabbed at his long tail, pulled him down and eaten him without anymore ado, bones and all. The only evidence was a few stray feathers that

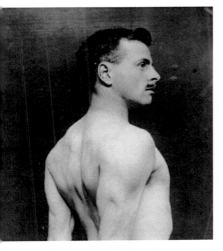

Before the Great War Dad ran
 body-building gym. Here he is
 n a classical pose which was
 probably used as an advertisement.

The photo of Mum that Dad took
with him when he went off to the
front.

Dad, Mum and Muriel in 1917.
What you can't see is the stick that
would have been behind the chair.
Having been badly wounded at
the Battle of the Somme, Dad
couldn't walk unaided until 1920.

Muriel with Frankie, the brother
I never knew. After he passed
away Mum had the photo framed
– having cut my sister out – and
it hung over her bed for the rest
of her life.

Dad outside the shop in Crewe which, as well as selling flowers, sold small animals and birds.

Dad with a beautiful blue Hyacinth macaw, the largest parrot in the world. Dad always wore a hat: a flat cap in the early days, then a trilby once we got to Upton.

Muriel and me at Shavington with a woolly monkey. Sadly I can now remember his name.

Babs holding her comfort blanket. She was the first chimp I knew and I loved to play with her when I was allowed to.

Canadian black bears at Shavington who I loved to talk to but who rarely took any notice of me.

This is the house at Shavington where I was born and where Dad and Granddad started 'The Oakfield Zoological Gardens'. By sheer chance the house that went on to become Chester Zoo was also called Oakfield.

Me, George and Mary.

Muriel was the oldest of the Mottershead cousins. Here we all are at Uncle Len's house in Sale, his daughter Mary is on the left, then it's me standing in front of Stanley, Paddy and George, Uncle Charlie's children.

George, Auntie Jessie, me and Stanley.

Me at Shavington. My knickers and socks were always hanging down.

Lulu, our ring-tailed lemur. Her fur was so soft that I loved to wear her round my neck like a scarf.

Granny at the pay box waiting for visitors. She always wore a jacket and a hat.

THE POLAR BEAR. CHESTER ZOOLOGICAL GARDENS. A10893.

Punch in his original pen looking his usual sad and bedraggled self. Before he arrived at the zoo he'd been in a travelling menagerie.

Visitors on the lawn in front of the big house with Muriel serving tea.

Me and my cousin George, who was my first love, with Granny and Granddad. Granny was rarely seen without her pinafore, Granddad rarely seen without his pipe.

Granddad and Granny outside the lodge at Oakfield. Although it was Granddad's second marriage, theirs was a true love match.

The entrance to the stable yard. On the right is the turret with the spiral staircase where Minnie the tapir got stuck.

Me with my first bike at the gate leading to the big orchard. I was really too young for a two-wheeler and fell off, gashing my forehead on the metal bell which left a scar for years.

The entrance to the Oakfield estate when my dad bought it.

Muriel and our first orphan lion cubs, which my sister reared by hand. They were donated by Miss Russell Allen. This was taken in the stable courtyard at Oakfield where all the animals were housed until 1938.

Dad with two orphan lion cubs. These two had been given to the Holt family as a gift from a Nigerian chief, and the Holts gave them to us.

Mary and me playing on the steps of the big house.

Granddad looked after everything to do with plants, from vegetables for us and the animals to eat, to hothouse orchids. He was already 78 when the zoo opened in 1931.

Granddad's beautiful conservatory which housed the reptiles as well as his tropical plants. To the right is the walk-through aviary with parrot cages on the wall.

Me, Mary and my doll's pram which we used to take turns in playing with, though I had really grown out of it by 1935.

Minnie our South American tapir was one of the first animals at the zoo. Here I am feeding her some of the windfalls from the orchard while Nora, the daughter of friends of my parents, has a ride.

Mary was a great copier. If I did something, she would want to do it too. Here she is drinking lemonade using a straw.

The wildfowl pool by the lodge I 'helped' Granddad dig,
which Granny later fell into, losing her second-best hat.

Dad with Christy and
Rob Rob in the room
where the parrots roosted
on cold nights, which
became our sitting room
after the war.

Lions are very susceptible
to infection when they're
little and here Dad is
checking that Christy is
gaining weight as she
ought to.

The day we first saw paper money! Look how excited we are.
Granddad, Granny, Dad, Muriel and me.

Me playing with two orphan lion cubs in the courtyard. Like kittens
they just want to play and a ball of string is as good a toy as anything.

Me in my school uniform with our first kinkajou, a nocturnal, rain-forest mammal related to lemurs.

Me giving a treat to Sammy, our second Malayan Sun bear. Sammy was a great escaper and was always giving us trouble.

Mary playing at washing clothes.

Dad building the new lion house in 1937, helped by Mary.

MOWGLI AND PETER

AT

CHESTER ZOO.

Mowgli the lion licking his friend Peter the terrier.
They really were inseparable.

Billy was given to the zoo at the outbreak of war as food for the lions but for some reason he was pardoned and he and I would play butting heads for hours. (And below).

Me and Rob Rob, our blue and red macaw. Although happy to stay in his cage while the zoo was open, he spent the rest of the time in the kitchen with us.

Birds flew freely in the walk-through aviary, an innovation for its time.

Me with Jet and Jet's puppy. The puppy went back to Miss Russell Allen, who bred Lilliputian terriers.

Visitors picnicking on the front lawn in the 1930s. We didn't mind if people brought their own food.

Dad in his trademark trilby with Peter the capybara, given to us by the Duke of Westminster, who was fed up of him escaping.

Lord Leverhulme places the foundation stone for the new lion enclosure. Standing between Dad and Lord Leverhulme is Charlie Collins, the zoo's first-ever employee. The glamorous lady on the left is Miss Geraldine Russell Allen, generous not only to the zoo but also to me.

Patrick in the new lion enclosure which was delayed by the war. It was the first time lions were kept behind fencing and not bars.

Unlikely friendships in the zoo included this ibis and a rabbit. The ibis enjoyed preening the rabbit's fur.

Won Lung and her new baby Belinda, the result of a mixed marriage between a Russian bear and a Himalayan bear.

Orphan babies needed to be bottle-fed just like human babies.

You have to be careful feeding pelicans and hold the fish by its tail so as not to be scratched by the hook on their beak.

My sister Muriel with an African porcupine she hand reared from a baby. It used to sit on her knee with all its quills sticking out to prevent anyone else muscling in.

Me teaching Mary to read.

Kiki and Tarzana. They were both very destructive so a new cage had to be built with very secure bars.

Patrick with two of his lionesses. He was a very nice lion and a very good father.

Our American bison Ferdinand (right) and his son Billy. Ferdinand came as an evacuee from Dudley Zoo and Billy was born at Chester. They were both as bad as each other. A piebald sheep is in the background.

Faith, Hope and Charity, who originally came from Bristol Zoo. Faith was Christy's grandmother.

'Kay' and his two elephants, Molly on the left, and Mannikin. This must have been taken shortly after he arrived at the zoo because Mannikin died soon afterwards.

Children loved riding on Molly, and the moment they got off they would queue up to go again.

Kay polishing Molly's toenails.

Ziggy, the Polish refugee, who took over as keeper from Muriel, with Solomon.

When he came to visit us after the war, Peter Scott was better known as a painter than a conservationist. Here he is with Christy and a zebra.

Sammy and Susie were unexpected arrivals in 1947. They proved great entertainment.

Ted Jarvis, a young keeper, with Belinda, our half-Russian, half-Canadian bear cub.

Me playing with Christy. Although I have my hand in her mouth she would never bite me.

Here I am proudly showing off my Girls Training Corp uniform. My Raleigh bicycle, complete with basket where Jet would ride, gave me freedom to visit my friends.

Won Lung and Trotsky in the foreground in their new enclosure.
Their favourite food was apples.

Punch and Judy
enjoying their
new pool. This is
where Fred
slipped in and
couldn't get out.

Former wartime
anti-tank road
blocks made
perfect supports
for the viewing
terrace above the
dens in the third
polar bear pool.

The entrance to the zoo showing the enlarged pay box and new car park.

A souvenir guidebook from the zoo. Our slogan was 'Always Building', and Dad certainly was!

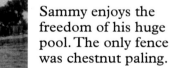

Sammy enjoys the freedom of his huge pool. The only fence was chestnut paling.

Fred Williams, Susie and Sammy in the polar bear pool when they first arrived – Punch and Judy were kept inside while the sea lions used the pool until their new one was ready.

Once I left the land army I returned to the zoo as keeper of the aquarium. Here I am collecting daphnia – food for my fish – our fallow deer Bambi keeping me company.

Muriel in her Wren uniform in 1944.

Christy and me on one of our daily walks around the grounds. I had hand reared her from one day old and she was the most beautiful lion cub I had ever seen.

Charlie Collins outside the reptile house which he built and then became its keeper. He was the only person allowed to drive the new van.

Ziggy wasn't only the chimp keeper, he also took visitors on rides around the wildfowl lake in our little motor boat and a chimp often went too.

Gerald Iles (centre), director of Belle Vue Zoo, who became a great friend of my father's (right). This photo was taken in the fifties but when I first met him in 1934 I thought him the most handsome man I had ever seen.

Fred and me shortly after our marriage. There was nothing Fred couldn't do and he became my dad's right-hand man.

Fred came to the zoo as a keeper. Here he is with Belinda, the daughter of Trotsky and Won Lung.

Punch, our original polar bear, clean for the first time in his life since moving to his new enclosure with a large pool, paid for by Miss Tomkyns Grafton who 'adopted' him in 1939.

The Happy Couple and a few others. . . Among them my great friend Nancy on the far right of the photo, standing next to Maud who was Muriel's great friend and who worked at the pay box. Next to her is Nancy's sister Margaret. Third from the left is my cousin Paddy looking very glamorous.

drifted around for weeks. A fox provided another unwitting meal when it bounded over his wall trying to escape from the local hunt.

Polar bears don't kill their prey. If they did that in the Arctic, it would freeze solid within minutes and they wouldn't be able to eat it anymore than we could if we took some meat straight from the freezer. Instead they just tear off the flesh bit by bit while it's still living, that way it keeps warm. Death by a lion or tiger would be easy in comparison. They would simply go for the throat and it would be over in seconds.

The bear enclosure was taking longer to finish than Dad had expected. It was the same old problem: lack of money. But something had to be done, that was clear.

Sally had more energy than any other animal in the zoo. But one morning one of the boys rushed into the kitchen saying that she'd gone. The former stables were only one storey high. Dad had given her branches to climb and, from that, she'd managed to make a hole in the roof. It turned out she hadn't gone far, but was just wandering across the tiles, taking the air.

Sally was always a great favourite with the visitors. As a former pet, she knew about doing tricks for rewards – preferably sweets or chocolate (her favourite food was condensed milk, which she sucked through a hole in the tin that one of us made). One day one of the boys left a bucket in her pen, and this became her favourite prop. She would sit in it, balance it on her head and do all manner of what in those days were called 'antics'. If everything else failed, she would roll on her back, paws in the air, until somebody threw her something she wanted. One day she managed to put the handle around her waist, and so it sat on her back like an elephant's howdah until, fortunately, the handle broke and it slipped off.

Animals were now flooding in. The Duke of Westminster donated his tame capybara. A capybara is the largest rodent in the world; it looks like a guinea pig, but is twice the size of a badger. His name was Peter and I grew very fond of him. He'd been living on an island in the middle of a lake in the grounds of the duke's estate, just south of Chester, called Eaton Hall. When the duke had installed him there, he hadn't realised what good swimmers capybaras are, and Peter was always escaping, which was why he was now coming to us. Peter wasn't happy unless he was chewing on something, so we always made sure there were plenty of logs to gnaw on, to keep his teeth down, as well as a pool, which he would sit in on warm days.

Another distinguished visitor was the Marquis of Tavistock, later the Duke of Bedford, who came to the zoo incognito and then presented us with a pair of rare black cockatoos.

The days of buying animals were over. New arrivals would either be donated or exchanged. Once the alligators in Granddad's conservatory grew too big, they were exchanged, replaced by two smaller ones exchanged for something else with a Dutch trader. Our exchange list always included a lot of parakeets and other birds because we bred so many. There was a poisonous snake that Dad had been given but didn't want. Later the list would always include lions, as the breeding programme was so successful. We got a llama this way, a rhea, a striped hyena, a dingo, an ocelot, a blacked-neck ibis. Two wallabies came from Dudley Zoo in exchange for two mandrills.

It was around this time that I first met Miss Esther Holt. I knew her name, of course; it was one you couldn't escape if you had anything to do with the zoo. She was the sister of Robert Holt, who ran the Holt Shipping Company – the Blue Funnel Line – and both she and her brother were major benefactors, not least by giving the zoo first refusal on the animals that were offered to them by Nigerian chiefs. This time her gift was more personal – her entire collection of 400 small tropical birds. Not only did she give them to the society, but she also paid for their upkeep. They lived mainly on tropical fruit, which would be delivered specially and which Muriel kept under lock and key in the pantry. It was the first time I'd seen pineapples, and I remember standing behind Mew, wrinkling my nose as she cut them up.

'Please, Mew! Just one small piece...'

'You're a pest, June. Go away.'

'But I don't know what it even tastes like!'

'Best you don't find out then, or you'll only want more.'

Another unexpected arrival was Cocky, a lemon-crested cockatoo. He wasn't a gift from an aristocrat or someone who'd got bored with him. He belonged to a lady who lived down the road in Upton. He was just too noisy, she explained, and the neighbours in her lodgings had complained to her landlord. She was even being threatened with eviction if she didn't do something about it. I have to admit that Cocky had a very forceful personality and was the loudest bird I have ever come across. 'Come and shake hands with Cocky!' he'd screech. If anyone asked his name, he'd spell it out: 'C-O-C-K-Y. Cocky!' This lady, who I remember as being very nice, used to visit the zoo twice a week to talk to him. He always knew when she was coming and would get very excited long before she had even got to the gate. He would bob up and down and display his beautiful yellow crest.

The zoo by this time had quite a collection of crowned cranes, the most famous of whom was Honky. Although he lived at the zoo, he didn't live in it, preferring to spend his days soaring around the countryside and just coming back to roost. One day Muriel took a call from Eaton Hall. Honky was making short work of the fish in his Grace's lake, they said, and could somebody please come and collect him. Eaton Hall was directly the other side of Chester – about eight miles as the crane flies – and as Dad was away, Muriel persuaded a council member who happened to be around to take her to collect him. Although this kindly man was fond of animals, neither he nor any of the duke's staff were prepared to help catch him and Muriel came back fuming, wet through to the skin. It was all probably a waste of time as Honky would have made his way back anyway once he'd decided he'd had enough. But the Duke of Westminster was an important person in the area and couldn't be ignored. Over the years Honky became a familiar sight within a radius of about fifteen miles of Oakfield. And then one day shortly after Easter in 1943, came another call. Honky had been gone for several days but no one was really worried, although by then he was nearly ten years old. Like all the other animals, his wartime diet was poor, but unlike the others he could supplement what he got at the zoo by his own

165

efforts. His body had been found near the estuary by someone who knew he 'belonged' to us. Poor Honky had no fear of humans and so must have approached his assassin thinking he might have some titbit to offer. He had been shot from a range of about ten feet and death would have been instantaneous.

Important visitors were becoming increasingly frequent, to the point where Granny found it difficult to know what to wear when she came up to the house, in case a chauffeur-driven car would turn up unexpectedly. Auntie Jessie, who had taken over from Granny at the pay box when she was living in the lodge, was regularly affronted when these cars, emblazoned with coats of arms, would sweep up the drive without stopping to pay! One was so shiny that the peacock thought he saw a rival in the door and began fighting his reflection and completely ruined the paintwork. From then on, he only had the courtyard to strut around. His days of liberty were over.

When Aunt Jessie left, Dad decided Granny shouldn't go back to her old job. She'd done enough, he said. Granny and Granddad were both nearer eighty than seventy and having a young family living under the same roof at their age can't have been easy. Normal children – which Stan, Paddy and George were – would be noisy. And while Granddad could get away and spend most of the time out in the garden, the lodge was Granny's home and she was very house-proud, everything always spick and span. Although she and Auntie Jessie got on perfectly well on the surface, I know there were tensions – there can't not have been. Granddad was a different matter. He got on well with everybody, he had that sort of placid personality. Many years later my cousin Paddy told me how, every day after lunch, they'd all have to be quiet or go out, as Granddad would be having his nap and couldn't be disturbed. He'd lie down on the settle, a cushion at both ends, and have forty winks. He'd just close his eyes and that would be that, she said. Half an hour later, he'd be back in the garden.

From then on, until the war, when she joined up, the pay box was run by Maud, a friend of my sister's. They had met doing 'music and movement', as it was called then, at Upton village hall, where the Women's League of Health and Beauty held classes. The photos of massed groups of young girls in identical white blouses and black satin shorts look a bit disturbing to our eyes now, too reminiscent of the rallies that were going on in Germany at the time, but it didn't feel like that then. There was very little in the way of leisure activities for girls of Mew's age. When I think about it now, her life was very hard. Until she met Maud, she hardly ever went out, because, apart from Marjorie, Dad's secretary, she didn't know anyone.

Marjorie Hayes had arrived in 1935, a year after the change to the North of England Zoological Society. She came from Bootle, in the heart of Liverpool's docklands, from a huge family. Like everyone else, she lived in the house – a room off Dad's office, which was on the first floor, in the servants' wing. Although a few years older than Mew, they soon became friends. I liked Marjorie because she was always kind to me and did things like looking after my tadpoles, though she wasn't so keen once they hatched and there were lots of little frogs hopping about. Marjorie was used to children – her sister Edna was about my age and would often come to stay, sometimes for weeks on end. Mum didn't seem to mind – animals or children or crippled soldiers, she couldn't shut the door on anyone.

Marjorie was very pretty and looked just like the Hollywood film star Myrna Loy. In fact she had a picture of her on her bedroom wall, taken with her regular co-star William Powell. She loved anything to do with Hollywood and every week, without fail, she would get her copy of *Picturegoer* from the paper shop, and all the old copies were stacked up in a corner for future reference. When Maud arrived, she, Marjorie and Mew became quite a threesome and would often go to the cinema together.

If council meetings were in the evening – which they usually were – Miss Russell Allen would insist that 'the young people' go to the cinema. Sam, her chauffeur, would be given the money to pay for everything – including an ice-cream in the interval. Then Charlie, Sammy, Billy, Nippy, Marjorie, Maud and Mew – whoever was around and not on duty that evening – would pile into her Bentley and off they'd go to the Majestic in Chester. Once the film had finished, he'd bring them back home. Unlike many of her kind, Miss Russell Allen was not only rich, she was thoughtful too.

I was too young to be included in these excursions and the only time I remember going to the pictures was once with Mum and Dad. I must have been about seven and we went to see *Trader Horn*, the true-life adventures of a big-game hunter and animal trader, and the first Hollywood film to be shot on location in Africa. Or so the advertising said, but I remember Dad spoiling it by complaining in a loud voice that macaws, which they had in the film, were not native to Africa but came from South America.

The only time I met a real big-game hunter was in May 1936, when Lady Delves Broughton came to open our fundraising fête. Although I had never heard of her, everyone else was very excited, especially my father. She lived at Doddington Hall, the other side of Northwich, with her husband Sir Henry 'Jock' Delves Broughton, but she was the more famous of the two – at least she was then – an excellent shot, they said, who had 'bagged' dozens of lions and leopards in Africa. She wasn't only adept with a gun, she went deep-sea fishing for tunny fish. Her husband's only claim to fame was a negative one – he'd been forced to sell thousands of acres of land that had been in his family for hundreds of years in order to settle gambling debts.

As usual with Dad, he recognised a good story when he saw it, and that afternoon the press were out in force. After she declared the fête open, my job was to present her ladyship with a basket of flowers, and disguised within it this time was her 'thank you' – a chameleon.

Before her arrival I'd imagined somebody dressed like the star of *Trader Horn*, wearing jodhpurs and a flimsy silk shirt, with tousled hair and generally looking very sultry and glamorous, but in fact she just looked haughty and rich. She had a pet Siamese gibbon called Miss Gibbs, whom she blamed for arriving late. All the photographers were rushing around getting pictures of Lady Delves Broughton and her pet, but I wasn't impressed. Our monkeys were just as nice. So why didn't they take photos of them?

Two years later she was in the news again, or rather her husband was. He was suspected of fraud, maintaining that a valuable pearl necklace of his wife's had been stolen and then claiming the insurance. But the real reason the Delves Broughton name has gone down in history was because of what happened in 1941. By this time they were divorced and Sir 'Jock' had married a young woman the same age as his daughter. To avoid a scandal, he and his new young wife had gone to live in Kenya, the area known as Happy Valley, where the new Lady Delves Broughton lost no time in starting an affair with the Earl of Erroll, another member of the decadent ex-pat community. When the earl was murdered, shot in the head in his car, 'Jock' Delves Broughton was arrested.

Although the trial was held in Nairobi, the British public followed every twist and turn, and that included the inhabitants of Oakfield. Charlie, Nippy and the other boys had been called up by then, and Mew was with the Wrens, so it was just me, Mum and Dad and a few new girls. By then fifteen, I was fascinated by such things as lovers, mistresses and murder, and was utterly gripped.

Not only was the accused a baronet whose family had lived in Cheshire for generations, he had given the zoo Miss Teeny, its third Malayan bear! And now our benefactor was on trial for his life. In Britain – and that included the colonies – to be found guilty of murder meant the death penalty. So we all knew that if the verdict went against him, he would hang.

We were then eighteen months into the war and life was hard. I suppose the trial helped take our minds off what was going on, things over which we had no control. It had all the ingredients a good murder ought to have. Lord Erroll had another lover who was famous for having a pet lion and who was never seen without a monkey on her shoulder. So perhaps she had done it out of spite.

Dad, of course, was in a special position, having known the accused personally. 'Is he the sort of man who could have murdered someone like that, in cold blood?' I asked him. He thought for a bit.

'Well, he was a gambler, so he had the necessary nerve and he was certainly reckless enough.'

The trial took place in Nairobi in June 1941, at a time when our corner of England was reeling from the damage done by the Luftwaffe. The Liverpool Blitz is not as well-known as the London Blitz, but Liverpool was where the convoys from America would come in – and it was the nerve centre of the whole North Atlantic operation. Food that came in to Liverpool from America was Britain's lifeline, which was why it was targeted. The May Blitz killed nearly 6,000 and wounded many more. Over 10,000 Liver-pudlians were made homeless. By June, while we were eagerly following the trial in the newspapers, there was what we thought was a bit of a lull in the raids. In fact it was the end of the worst, as Hitler had by then turned his attention to Russia with Operation Barbarossa, and apart from one or two nights the following Christmas, the raids on Liverpool stopped.

Sir Henry 'Jock' Delves Broughton was acquitted, the evidence being inconclusive, the jury decided. But less than a year later, he committed suicide, so who knows what that meant.

Our second Malayan bear was called Sammy, and he arrived the moment the new enclosure was finished, in the autumn of 1936, as an exchange with another zoo. He was much bigger than Sally, but they seemed to get on reasonably well. A photo taken the day they moved in shows a grassy field and a tree in full leaf. That didn't last long. The first thing they did was to strip the oak tree. It's still there to this day – its bare branches a reminder of what animals can do if they have a mind to. But the tree served its purpose as far as the public was concerned. Both bears loved wrestling and Sammy, being bigger, would usually win, sending Sally scuttling up the tree. As for the grassy floor, it was soon a sea of mud, though they didn't seem to care. As long as they could forage for worms and burrow, they were happy.

The Delves Broughton bear, Miss Teeny, arrived two years later, shortly before their divorce, and I wonder now, given the similarity of the names, if she'd been a pet of Lady Delves Broughton that had nowhere to go when the marriage ended. Unlike her Siamese gibbon, Miss Gibbs, a bear wasn't portable.

Even so, Miss Teeny was much smaller than Sally and only a quarter the size of Sammy, who seemed to grow a few inches every week. When she was first introduced into the enclosure there was concern over how Sally and Sammy would react to the newcomer. We needn't have worried. To Sally's obvious annoyance, Sammy fell in love with her straight away, and Sally just had to put up with it.

Early one morning, before the household was really awake, Rob Rob gave a loud screech from the kitchen. This was his usual warning that something out of the ordinary was happening. I was still in bed, but the squawk was so loud that I got up and looked out of the window to find out what the commotion was. All I could see was Mew and Charlie racing across the lawn towards Granddad's vegetable garden. I grabbed my dressing gown and ran downstairs and out of the garden door, to see Sammy walking calmly along the top of the garden wall. Mew and one of the boys were looking up at him. Then Dad came out carrying his shotgun.

'Back in the house,' Dad said when he saw me. 'I've got enough on my plate here without worrying about you.'

Of course he was right. Bears are never safe, and when cornered – as Sammy was now – they are doubly dangerous. I went back upstairs, not to Mew's and my bedroom, but the parrots' room, which had a better view. I was just in time to see Sammy drop down off the wall into the garden. My heart sank. If he could make such a mess of his own compound, where there was nothing to eat, what would he do with Granddad's vegetables? And what if he discovered the auriculas? Luckily Granddad himself wasn't there.

It was decided to keep Sammy contained there until someone came up with a strategy. From time to time his furry head would appear over the top of the wall, but the boys were patrolling the outside and they'd threaten him with a stick and he'd duck back down again. He even managed to get onto the roof of Punch's den, but was driven back into the garden. Meanwhile someone had brought a travelling crate up to the garden door in the back yard. Then Dad and one of the boys, armed with clothes props from the washing line, went in and, encouraged by a tin of condensed milk, Sammy got the message.

Carl Hagenbeck's measurements had been very exact, and for nearly three years the wall had been high enough, but in the meantime Sammy had grown, and that night, he'd dislodged the iron rod that barred the door and, once free, had scaled the concrete wall to make good his escape. There was drainage work going on at the time – an attempt to do something about the quagmire they had churned up – and so the bears were being kept inside the den longer than was usually the case, and Sammy obviously didn't like it. It turned out that he'd grown over a foot since he'd arrived, so in addition to the new drain, another layer was added to the wall, which can still be seen.

However, no sooner was everyone back at work than the alarm was raised again! Less than half an hour had passed since he'd gone back in, but he'd now got a taste for freedom and there was no stopping him. Just like before, he'd climbed up the wall, but had gone in a different direction, and in a few minutes he had left the zoo grounds completely, heading down a back lane. I had left for school by this time, but Charlie told me all about it when I got back.

The chase had gone on for about half an hour when Sammy decided to climb a tree and have a rest. No amount of persuasion would get him down. One of the boys shinned up another tree beside it and tried to poke him down with a clothes prop, but he wouldn't budge. Dad decided he needed a shock and, hearing a lorry stop somewhere further up the lane, went up and asked the driver to do him a favour and drive past the tree, making as much noise as he could. The driver was a bit bemused, but agreed, and in a few minutes the lorry approached Sammy's tree, engine whining, horn honking, gears grinding, brakes screeching. It did the trick.

The terrifying behaviour of this 'mechanical monster', as Dad called it, sent Sammy scrambling down the tree and off in the direction of home like a shot.

Chapter 7

At the start of 1938 there seemed to be light at the end of the tunnel. Although there was no money in reserve, the previous year's takings, both through the gate and at the café, were higher than they ever had been. There was now a regular bus service from Chester – run by Crosville, the company who had put on the Crewe/Shavington service. This would make a huge difference to ordinary visitors. At that time, very few working people had cars. At the other end of the social spectrum, membership of the society was rising, not dramatically, but consistently, although with the stock of animals at a high, costs were also rising. A new animal nearly always meant a new pen. A new pen meant additional duties for the keepers.

Eight weeks earlier our two mandrills, Sarah and George – highly coloured baboons that had come to us through the Holts – had produced a baby girl called Dawn. She arrived out of the blue – nobody had realised Sarah was even expecting. She was the first mandrill ever to be born in captivity in Britain and was doing well. Easter 1938 saw record crowds, which the zoo needed after struggling through the winter with a large stock of animals – we now had fifty monkeys across fifteen different species, for example.

Mary the chimp had been on her own since her arrival in 1931. She was very special to everyone: Mew because she'd reared her, me because she was my friend, and everyone else because she'd been with us from the very beginning. She was both sweet-natured and very clever. She could tie a knot better than I could, and one afternoon, when it was raining, I went into her pen to teach her how to do cat's cradle with a loop of wool. It was the current fad at school. Girls were doing it everywhere, on the bus, in the playground, under their desks, but no one else, I thought smugly, was doing it in a chimp house. We were sitting together on a bed of straw and I'd made her a loop of her own and she was doing her best to copy me, but it is quite difficult and you need great control of fingers and thumbs. I must have been hidden from view, or Mum was distracted, because she came along, found the cage unlocked and bolted it. I was so engrossed in what we were doing that I didn't even notice. It was only when she came back to do her rounds that she found me. Poor Mum was mortified and let me have a banana mashed up in top-of-the-milk.

Visitors love chimpanzees and Dad always knew that he wanted more. Not for breeding purposes, at least not then – a female doesn't have her first baby until she's about twelve or thirteen – but just because chimps are naturally gregarious and enjoy each other's company and in the wild they live in large colonies.

Tarzana had arrived in Liverpool in May 1935, with another female chimp called Silver Jubilee, named in commemoration of George V celebrating twenty-five years on the throne. Silver Jubilee was very sweet-natured, but she didn't stay long and was exchanged for a llama.

Tarzana was the most unreliable chimpanzee in the zoo and Mary was always wary of her. Had she been human, you'd have called Tarzana 'highly strung', and she had been like that since she'd arrived. Dad had gone up in the car to collect a consignment of animals from Liverpool docks – they'd come courtesy of the Holts. And somehow, with all that was going on, she had escaped.

Tarzana wasn't as young as Mary had been when she'd arrived – she was possibly three or four. Nobody knew her background, but, like Mary, she would have been captured when her mother was killed. If she had been taken as a baby and lived as someone's pet for a few years before being shipped to England, the separation from her adopted family would have been bad enough. But if she had witnessed the slaughter of her mother more recently, at an age when she knew what was happening, she would have been traumatised. By the time she was being carried down the gangplank at Liverpool, she would have been highly stressed.

In the 1930s the Mersey was known as 'the world's greatest maritime highway'. Sometimes, when Dad was collecting just one animal from a sailor, I would go with him. There were cranes and derricks everywhere, cargo being winched up from the holds in vast nets, swinging wildly as the contents were hoisted into the air, trains throwing out steam and soot, grunting and clacking as they left the dockside loaded up with bananas. And the noise – hooting, shouting, crashing, banging – was nonstop. Chimps don't like loud noises, especially noises they don't understand, and after the comparative calm of life on board the ship, with sailors no doubt making a fuss of her, it must have been terrifying.

I never found out quite what happened – whether she jumped from the arms of whoever was carrying her before they reached the quay, or whether it was after they got to Dad's car. But at some point she leapt. Chimps are agile and strong. They are equally as quick on the ground or when climbing, and Tarzana already had a reputation as an acrobat, hence her name. Eventually, after several hours at liberty, she was caught. Liverpool was the banana capital of England. Ships would be full of nothing else and they'd be brought up in leather buckets on conveyor hoists. Even so, a ship would take three days to fully unload. Most would go straight onto trains, which would then disperse across the country, but some were warehoused. Bananas have a strong, pungent smell and, being a favourite food with chimpanzees, it must have reminded her of home. And that's where she was finally cornered – in a banana warehouse. She would need very careful handling for quite a long time, Dad warned when he got back. She had been in a terrible state when he finally got her in the car.

Although she appeared to settle down reasonably quickly once in her new home, Mary gave her a wide berth, and that was very rare as she was affectionate and generous to anyone, human or animal. Visitors never really took to Tarzana either; they seemed to sense in her something broken. However, when Kiki arrived the following October, she and Tarzana bonded like a couple of naughty kids. Kiki came from the Congo rather than Nigeria. She had a black face and walked like a gorilla and used to beat her chest, something the other chimps never did, and she was certainly much stronger. She was a different breed, Dad said, and very rare; the only other one in captivity was in Berlin.

Kiki had grown up having the freedom of a compound near Katanga where her owner, Mr Hyde, ran a rubber plantation. But one day she'd absconded, disappearing for six months, before turning up in a local village. Having spent all her life with humans, she hadn't been able to settle in the wild. These villagers didn't want her – her name meant 'bad woman' in their language – and neither now did Mr Hyde. The Depression had hit everywhere, including the Congo, so he had come back to England, bringing Kiki with him, as well as a pair of mandrills, which Dad exchanged with Mr Greed for the three lionesses.

Kiki and Tarzana would egg each other on and generally cause as much trouble as they could. Tarzana would worry the screws in her cage until she got them loose and then try to take them out with a piece of bent metal which she would hide when she thought anyone was watching, while Kiki used brute strength, throwing her weight at the mesh and rocking it so that the supports gave way.

It didn't help when visitors broke the rules. There was a six-foot gap between the wall, behind which people stood, and the pen. One day a young man climbed over, claiming later that he had dropped his handkerchief on the other side and needed to pick it up. Before he knew what had happened, a hand came out and grabbed his coat. Belatedly realising the danger he could be in, he quickly slipped it off and Kiki was soon parading around wearing her trophy. She then started searching through the pockets and, finding a roll of developed film, peered at the negatives as if she were an expert in photography. In the meantime Tarzana – who never liked to be upstaged – attempted to grab the coat for herself, which resulted in a tug of war. When the coat got ripped they decided to share it, and tore it in half. Meanwhile a substantial crowd had gathered and thoroughly enjoyed the performance, which everyone agreed was the funniest thing they had ever seen. It was talked about for years. All the young man could do was stand and watch.

It was clear that the chimpanzees needed somewhere stronger to contain them, and reluctantly Dad accepted that this would need bars. It would be nearly another twenty years before his ground-breaking chimp islands were inaugurated, in 1956, when he took a gamble that the one thing chimpanzees couldn't do was swim.

On 29 January 1938 there was a special benefit day to raise money for the new chimp house, and he'd made a model of it, showing both the indoor and outdoor accommodation. As he said in his speech, although chimpanzees were the 'star turn' and the zoo was dependent on them, they were becoming a 'real handful' and were in desperate need of more space. Earlier in the afternoon, the recent extension to the aquarium was opened – this contained our first tropical tanks, bringing the total up to ten. To drink there was a fruit punch, but my job was just to hand round cheese straws and fiddly titbits for humans. We raised a considerable amount that day: donations varied from a few shillings to £50.

The existing chimp pens were at the far side of what had been the stables, and by blocking up the end and enclosing a part of the courtyard, Dad realised a sturdier and much larger pen could be made. But chimps are creatures of habit and they were even unsettled when other animals moved pens. So he feared that, even though they were doing their best to destroy their current home, when it came to it, there might be hell to pay.

The new building had a concrete floor with hot-water pipes running through it. Until then, heating had been a problem. Only a brick wall separated the new quarters from the old, so it was just a question of knocking through. And Dad had a plan. Mary had loved helping him with the building work, shouldn't Kiki and Tarzana be the same? The ruse worked perfectly. Once the first brick had been dislodged and fallen out on their side, Kiki and Tarzana took over, refusing to let anyone approach, and everyone working on the other side took the hint. In a matter of minutes, the two chimps had made a hole large enough to get through. Once inside, they proceeded to inspect their new home carefully – every bar was tested by putting their entire weight on it using their feet. All the nuts were examined, the back door tried and opened. When safely through, and the door locked, Mary was ushered into the two tearaways' former quarters, and Dad and the others watched her reaction carefully. First she peered through the hole and then eyed up the bricks on the floor. Next, before barely a minute had passed, she began bricking the hole up again. When the bricks wouldn't fit, where the old mortar hadn't come off, she began trimming them with a mallet. The bricks were painted green on one side, and she made sure that they were put back the right way round. Once she'd fitted them in, she gathered up the crumbly old mortar from the floor and pushed it into the cracks. She knew what she was doing because she'd 'helped' Dad and Charlie build the lion house a short while before. How useful she really was, I'll never know, because it was one of Dad's publicity exercises. At the beginning she was probably just there for the photographers, but Mary had always been a quick learner and enjoyed copying what people did, and I remember coming back from school and seeing her trowelling on the cement between the courses of bricks

186

and then adding the next layer.

That June, I went with my father to collect a consignment of animals from Portland in Dorset. The year before, I had gone with him to Dudley Zoo shortly after it had opened. It was my birthday treat.

The Blue Funnel Line didn't only dock at Liverpool, it also made regular trips to Rotterdam in Holland. But if there was a consignment of animals for Chester Zoo, the Holts would arrange for a pilot boat to bring them off at Portland. It was better that they came straight to us, rather than spending six months being quarantined in Holland.

We set off from Chester on the afternoon of my twelfth birthday and it took hours, even though, compared to today, the roads were empty. I think I must have slept on the journey, but I know Dad drove through the night, because he always did. I would drift off to him singing 'Roses of Picardy' and 'Girls Were Made to Love and Kiss'. When we finally got there, we were told there was a change of plan. We'd have to wait, as the King, George VI, was reviewing the fleet.

We stayed overnight in a bed and breakfast on Portland Bill, and the next morning we watched from the cliffs near the lighthouse. A review of the fleet is not something that happens all the time, but there had been rumblings of trouble across Europe since early in the year, and in March Germany had invaded Austria. The Royal Navy was the most powerful in the world, and this was a show of strength to remind those who seemed to have forgotten – namely Germany and Italy – that Britain was a force to be reckoned with.

The King was there, the Duke of Kent was there, Lord Mountbatten was there. The sea was crowded with battleships, cruisers and destroyers. As a spectacle, it was just fantastic and I will never forget it. A wireless-controlled plane was sent up and then fired on and came twisting down in smoke into the sea, and around us everyone cheered. To me then, it just seemed exciting – like hitting the target with the bow and arrow Granddad had made me. Although the sun was sparkling on the water, the grey of all those ships coloured everything. One of them was HMS *Courageous,* an old First World War battle cruiser which had been converted into an aircraft carrier to do convoy duty across the Atlantic. It was torpedoed by a German U-boat in the Western Approaches in September 1939, just two weeks after war was declared. Of her crew of 1,260 – including air force officers, 519 lives were lost, as well as 38 planes. When we heard the news in those first terrifying days of the war, Dad and I both remembered the name and looked at each other. It had been announced that the King had gone on

188

board the HMS *Courageous* for a concert, and Dad had had to explain to me what an aircraft carrier was. In the years that followed I used to wonder sometimes how many of the ships I'd seen out there on that beautiful sunny day never came back.

The next morning Dad went out with the pilot to collect the animals from the Blue Funnel Line ship that was lying at anchor. We set off home to Chester as soon as he got back. There was a chimp, whose name I've now forgotten, who had been seasick. There were two crowned cranes and a vervet monkey, as well as a couple of African grey parrots, plus a box of reptiles of some description. Somehow they were all crammed into our boxy little Hillman Minx. I wanted to hold the chimp, but Dad wouldn't let me. He usually did these journeys on his own and as I was taking up the passenger seat, I had to have a parrot cage on my knee. Dad put the crowned cranes in sacks, with holes cut for their heads and cord tied round their tail feathers to stop them from getting bashed about, and because they were so tall – even though they were young – they went in the well in front of the back seat, to give them extra height. The chimp went in a small travelling crate which perched on top of the boxes containing the reptiles. In that way, he had a view out of the window to keep him occupied. The monkey was next to him on the back seat.

Although this particular trip was a special treat for me, basically it was normal life. Dad was always coming back with the car full of animals, so it didn't strike me as being anything very unusual. But on the journey back I saw the shock on people's faces whenever we stopped – mostly just for petrol. It was only when you went outside our world that you realised life at the zoo was so different to everyone else's. As a child, I had just accepted things as they were. Of course you played with chimps, why wouldn't you? Of course you knew the difference between a gibbon and a baboon, or a crocodile and an alligator. It was like the difference between a cart horse and a pony. Or a goat and a sheep. It was obvious.

As far as my parents were concerned, everything was possible. 'It can be done' was one of my dad's favourite phrases. Another was, 'It's just common sense.' But looking back at it all now, I realise that the risks he took were enormous. On one occasion he took the ferry across to Dublin to pick up some snakes. Not wanting to leave them in the car on the way back, he brought up the wicker laundry basket they were travelling in and had them on deck. When he went inside to get something to eat, he left them there, and when he came back, two nuns were sitting on it having a sandwich...

In September 1938 Dad had a phone call from Lewis's, the big Liverpool department store. They had a small Russian bear they couldn't sell, they said, and if Mr Mottershead was prepared to collect it, he could have it. With the prospect of war looming over Europe, the appetite for exotic animals had disappeared, the manager explained. Now he just wanted it to go to a good home.

On the night of 29 September 1938 Germany, Britain, France and Italy had signed the Munich Pact – Chamberlain's famous 'peace for our time'. In effect, it gave Hitler permission to annex the German-speaking part of Czechoslovakia. Not only was this western region of the country of strategic importance – its defences were there – but it was economically important too, the bulk of its heavy industry was also there.

That evening Dad retold the story of having to collect Adam and Eve, the Canadian black bears, as the boys hadn't heard it. Adam had died of old age in 1934, around the time the society took over running the zoo. Eve had been distraught at the loss of her mate and whined pitifully for hours on end. A few months later, he'd got in another Canadian bear, but she wasn't interested. Although Dad considered him 'very handsome and a very fine specimen', Eve wasn't to be persuaded. She put up with him, but that was all, and at some point he was exchanged. A hyena was then put in next door, but another bear would be a much better companion, Dad decided. We christened the new bear Trotsky, after the renegade communist who had been exiled from the Soviet Union and was then living in Mexico. He would be assassinated in 1940.

Trotsky the bear was very young and, comparatively speaking, Eve was an old lady, but there was no obvious antagonism. So one day the doors between their two cages were raised to see what happened. Trotsky went in, brimming with confidence, wanting to play. Eve made a lunge at him, snarling viciously, but only dealt him a gentle cuff before backing away. She didn't want to hurt him – she could easily have done so, being then about four times his size – it was just a friendly warning not to push his luck. But, all in all, it was decided to leave the interconnecting doors open. Sometimes Trotsky would seem to forget that Eve existed, but when she crept up behind him in readiness for a spring, he would turn quickly and fasten her in a clinch, only releasing her when she had worked herself up into a rage. At night he would climb up on top of Eve's den and settle down to sleep, with his nose drooping over her doorway. He had a perfectly good den himself, but he preferred to stay where he was.

The winter of 1938/9 was very cold and we lost several of the animals, including some monkeys and my old friend Minnie the South American tapir. Animals died all the time, but on the whole it was more like a cow or a sheep dying on a farm – more of a blow financially than emotionally. But the death of someone like Minnie was upsetting, and not only to me. She was a determined and decided character who had been part of the zoo since we first opened. However, she made it clear in everything she did that she was here of her own volition and the decision to live at the zoo was her choice not ours. And of course as Minnie was so big and died in the winter when the ground was hard, it took much more of an effort to dig her grave. I would usually hold a small ceremony, but because the orchard – where animals were usually buried – would never be dug up or built on, the place was generally not marked in any formal way, except by me sometimes – as in the case of Minnie – with a small cairn of stones. But it was very sad. I would go into the courtyard and expect to see her snuffling around, with the monkeys teasing her, and then I would remember.

During the Christmas holidays I spent most of my time in the aquarium. We now had a fulltime aquarist called Peter Falwasser. He loved what he did and was happy to share his knowledge with me, and any spare time I had, I'd be down there. At first the only thing he let me do was to clean the glass on the tanks, inside and out. Not the most exciting job, but important. Eventually he let me help with furnishing the tanks, choosing pebbles and gravel and using small rocks to create caves and bridges that the fish could swim in and out of.

Peter's enthusiasm was infectious and I was soon fascinated. Some fish had their young live and would protect them by keeping them in their mouths. The baby fish would swim near their mother and, at the first sign of danger, they'd swim back in. Some fish created nests in the gravel and would take as much care of the eggs as birds did. There were also the bubble-nest breeders, such as Siamese fighting fish, where the male would squeeze the eggs out of the female, catch them in his mouth, then take them up to the bubble nest he had already created on the surface of the water. Only then would he fertilize them.

My favourite fish were the freshwater angelfish from the Amazon, simply because they were so graceful. The prettiest were the neon tetras, with their iridescent blue bodies and bright-red tails. The most bizarre-looking were the elephantnose fish from West Africa, which have the largest brain-to-body-weight ratio of all known vertebrates. The male Siamese fighting fish were particularly splendid, with their long, flowing, brightly coloured fins and tails. They were at their best when displaying to females, but sometimes we'd put a mirror in the corner of the tank and they would show off to their own reflections. Fish, unlike most animals in captivity, turned out to be very easy to breed, which would serve us well.

During the week I wasn't allowed to work in the aquarium because Mum said my homework was more important, but I was completely hooked and Peter relied on me to make infusoria – aquatic microorganisms – to give to the newly hatched fish.

In the autumn of 1937 Dad had started a newsletter called *Zoo News*. Originally it was just for members, to bring them up to date with what was happening, but it proved so popular that it was extended to anyone who wanted to subscribe, and copies were available at the pay box and at the till for the café. At the end of 1938 Dad had launched yet another appeal for more members and donations. Over the last four years, since the zoo had been run on its current lines as the North of England Zoological Society, 111,000 people had come through the gates. At first glance it might have looked impressive, but to put it in perspective, it was fewer than the numbers that went to

Regent's Park over one Whitsun weekend ten years earlier. Something had to happen.

April 1939 saw the long-hoped-for arrival of a male lion, in exchange for two young lionesses that Muriel had reared from cubs, the ones who had come from a Nigerian chief. Patrick was six years old and came from Dublin, hence the name. Everyone just held their breath that one or other of our three lionesses would take his fancy. Patrick was put in an adjoining cage and Faith, Hope and Charity entered with trepidation. They had heard him and smelled him. They entered warily, their noses high, suspicious and tense. Males look quite different from females and they were only three years old. We didn't know if they had even seen an adult male lion before, and Patrick was particularly magnificent, in the prime of life, looking like a story-book picture of a lion, all shaggy mane and fine-featured, intelligent face. Suddenly there was a terrifying roar when the newcomer was spotted in the adjoining cage. The three lionesses became very agitated – careering round their cage, leaping high in the air. My father called it 'a spectacle of jungle fury' as they snarled and spat, their faces contorted with rage. Suddenly they bolted back to their den, he said, only to return with redoubled fury at the interloper who had dared come next door.

Meanwhile Patrick himself was unmoved.

The ferry crossing from Dublin had not been smooth and, according to his keeper, he was still feeling under the weather. Eventually the lionesses calmed down, sprawling out in one corner of their cage and making the occasional roar. Patrick did nothing but feel sorry for himself.

The next morning, feeling better, he seemed to have devised a strategy. He carried a meaty bone towards the mesh that separated them, put it down and retreated a few feet. The lionesses put paws through in an effort to reach it, but of course they couldn't, because the wire was in between. This generous gesture appeared to have done the trick, though, and the hostile atmosphere cleared. Relief all round.

Within a month Patrick had made his choice. It was Faith, and he was soon standing behind her while she was eating, to protect her from danger, allowing her to eat her meal first. Her cubs would be the first to be born at the zoo.

There was much to celebrate that spring. After seven years of trying, the griffon vultures had at last succeeded in hatching and rearing a healthy chick. Each year, since they'd arrived from Shavington, the female would lay an egg. One year it was coddled. One year they just ate it. One year the egg rolled off and broke. One year it hatched, but the chick was washed away in a storm.

No wonder everyone was so happy. It was the first time a griffon vulture had been reared successfully in captivity.

To cap it all, over 1,000 visitors came to the zoo on Whit Monday. I have no idea how we coped in the café, although many people brought picnics, but even with extra staff we were run off our feet. I was making trips out to Granddad for 'More lettuces!' and 'More radishes!' and 'More tomatoes!' Charlie was despatched up to the farm for more milk for the teas. Mr Dean was called for more bread. And still they kept coming. The car park was full. Charabancs came from far away, and local buses arrived with standing-room only. There were babies in prams and pushchairs, and toddlers taking their first steps in reins.

The Malayan bears had been joined now by a fourth, called Roger, who had arrived from Liverpool Zoo when it closed late in 1938. He wasn't used to all the attention, and while Sally did her usual tricks and was rewarded in the usual way, he just stood there looking lost. But the spectators so loved them all that they showered him with sweets anyway.

As for the chimps, Jimmy, our newest baby – then two years old – swung high on his trapeze and did backward somersaults, clearly loving the attention. Some of the children had never seen a chimp before and stood watching him, entranced. I didn't see any of this myself. I was too busy in the kitchen and the café and looking after the till. But I have a press cutting from the *Chester Chronicle* that describes it vividly. In a later paragraph the reporter says he was sorry not to have seen Mary on better form. He had obviously been to the zoo before, and knew what she was like, and how normally she would have loved the crowds, especially the children. The writer quotes 'the Curator, Mr Mottershead' as saying that Mary was suffering from melancholia. She wasn't. She was suffering from bronchitis, which she had probably caught from a human visitor.

Muriel did what she could, but we all knew that Mary's chances of recovery were slim. There wasn't much you could do with a sick chimp back then, just nurse her, give her warm milk, rub her chest with Vicks vapour rub, keep her comfortable. And hope. I hoped that once the warm weather arrived, she would get better. But she didn't. The bronchitis turned into pneumonia and Mary died on 30 June 1939, a week after my thirteenth birthday. She was only nine – a youngster in chimp terms.

Her death was announced in *Zoo News*, together with an account of her life. An obituary, I suppose you could call it. And that was fitting. There were other chimps – Jimmy comes to mind, sweet-natured and very good-looking – but no one would ever replace Mary in my affections, because she was my friend at a time when I had no other. She was generous and never jealous – even of Jimmy. If she thought he was getting more attention, she would just clap her hands and do something to get your notice, something funny and endearing.

For the last few years we had spent less time in each other's company, but that was only to be expected. It didn't mean that I had stopped caring. We had grown up together, but as you grow up, you grow out of people, including chimps.

I know I am lucky to have had her friendship. And thanks to all those photographs that the press had taken – Mary and me playing with my doll's pram, Mary and me walking along hand in hand, Mary and me just holding onto each other and laughing – I will never forget her as long as I live.

Chapter 8

In the edition of *Zoo News* that followed the Munich Agreement in September 1938, my dad expressed his gratitude to Mr Chamberlain for signing the pact. The shadow of war, he wrote, had threatened the zoo with what might have been its utter destruction.

Everyone knows that in the event of war zoos have to reduce their stocks considerably, on account of feeding, but modern warfare today would have presented far greater difficulties and the moment might easily have arrived when for sheer safety's sake and humane consideration, we would have been called upon to shoot the animals to which we are so attached. That we have been spared the horrors of war makes us so thankful that we must not grumble at the enormous loss the mere threat of it has cost the zoo.

But as the months went by it became clear to him, as it did to thousands of others, that what Chamberlain had secured was not 'peace for our time' but only breathing space. And when Hitler marched into Poland on 1 September 1939, Dad knew the game was up.

Two days later we all gathered around the radio in the kitchen to listen to the prime minister address the nation. Even though I was only thirteen, I will never forget it. Even now it sends chills down my spine.

I am speaking to you from the cabinet room at 10 Downing Street. This morning the British Ambassador in Berlin handed the German government a final note stating that, unless they were prepared to withdraw their troops from Poland, a state of war would exist between us. I have to tell you now that no such undertaking has been received and that consequently we are at war with Germany.

It was eleven o'clock in the morning and a beautiful late-summer's day – a Sunday – and we should have been expecting a good turnout of visitors, as it was the perfect weather for a trip to the zoo. That morning it had been as if Mum was sleepwalking. When you spoke to her, or asked her a question, she just looked vacant and didn't reply. So we had buttered the bread as usual and prepared the salads and got out the ham and the cheese. I'd gone to fetch radishes and cucumbers from the greenhouse and Granddad had just been sitting on a bench smoking his pipe. He didn't say anything either.

Although war had always been there in the

background – the uncles who never came back, my two grandmothers both having lost their sons, the men who tramped the roads and begged for food – I had no real sense of what it meant. But my parents did. Twenty-one years – which was all it was since the Armistice in November 1918 – was no time at all in their lives. And it was meant to be the war to end all wars.

When the broadcast ended Mum got up and went out, closing the door quietly behind her, and I heard her footsteps echoing upstairs. Dad clasped his hands on his knees and looked around at the boys. They were all about twenty-one then – well over the minimum age for call-up.

'So what happens now, Mr Mott?' one of them blurted out.

'Well, I don't see zoo keepers being considered a reserved occupation essential to the war effort,' he said. 'But until we know the drill, it's business as usual.'

'But what about the animals?' I asked him later as we walked across to see Granddad, who'd gone back to the lodge to listen to the broadcast with Granny. 'Who's going to look after them after the boys have gone?'

'We'll advertise for some young women,' he said. 'And they'll do very well, mark my words. Look at Mew – she's the best keeper we've got. There's nothing the boys can do that she can't. And you can't say the same vice versa.'

'So Mew's staying here?'

'Of course she is. There are no plans to call up young women.'

And there weren't, not then.

But we did lose Mew. Within less than a month she had signed up as a volunteer. I too had seen the posters by the bus stop: 'Join the Wrens – free a man for the fleet.' In fact I think it was her own freedom she was looking for. She was going on a great adventure and I was really happy for her. I knew I would miss her, but the truth was, our lives didn't interconnect that much. Ten years is a huge gap between sisters, and Mew was really a different generation to me. I was at school and she was working. Although her usual term of endearment was 'pest', I knew she didn't really mean it and, as for me, I utterly revered her. She had an instinct with animals that I knew I would never have in a million years.

My father was the most inventive person I have ever known. If a problem needed solving, he'd find the answer. If it worked, then good. If it didn't, he'd try again. And again, and again. He never gave up.

He was facing real concerns in terms of the animals, but he'd had a year now to think about it. Liverpool Zoo, run by his friend Captain Rogers – one of the original investors in the Chester Zoological Society – had closed shortly after Munich because Captain Rogers had no confidence in the future. We had even taken some of the animals, including Roger, our fourth Malayan bear.

Now the newspapers were full of stories about animals being shot. And it was true that food would be a problem. Given the country didn't produce enough to feed itself, all non-essential consumption had to be weighed up.

'Too many people have got the jitters,' Dad wrote in the October 1939 issue of *Zoo News*, 'rather than staying calm and acting with judgment.' His view was that whether or not you considered the humanitarian perspective, if animals were destroyed it would be difficult – in some cases impossible – to replace them. But in the meantime they had to be fed.

Feeding the carnivores was the most difficult, particularly the lions. They needed huge quantities of meat a day – somewhere between nine and fifteen pounds, depending on their weight and the time of year. Luckily horsemeat was still available, as the suppliers' usual markets – Belgium and France – would shortly disappear. Local abattoirs were contacted for anything that wasn't considered fit for human consumption – offal, lights (lungs), poultry heads and carcasses, and particularly meaty cattle bones, which not only gave the lions calcium to maintain their teeth and gums in good condition, but also kept them occupied. Above all, the meat had to be raw and completely fresh, otherwise it lacked essential amino acids they needed for their eyesight.

Horses and goats whose owners felt they could no longer look after them were accepted by the zoo for use as and when required. Their animals would be cared for, Dad emphasised, with as much consideration and kindness as the exhibits. And they were. One who had been accepted on this basis – a goat named Billy – was 'pardoned' and became a much-loved character at Oakfield, though why he in particular was spared, I haven't a clue. Billy loved pretending to butt my head, and he and I would square up and run towards each other, one each side of the fence, time after time, and he soon became a great favourite with the visitors.

Although carnivores were the most expensive animals to feed, herbivores that originated in the tropics could be equally costly – fruit- and nut-eating birds being the obvious example. Local grocers did what they could by saving us damaged fruit and broken biscuits, which Dad would collect each day.

Although I have no proof – and never will – Dad's idea for animal adoptions may well have come thanks to Miss Holt's collection of tropical birds that she'd donated several years earlier. Although they were in the zoo, she paid for their food. So why shouldn't the same apply to other animals?

Whether the plan had been simmering for several weeks, or even months, or whether it was one of my father's eureka moments – that bulb that would light up in his head at a moment of crisis – I will never know. But within two weeks of war being declared, Dad's 'adoption scheme' was in place, and newspapers across the country were more than happy to give it coverage. It seemed measured and sensible – a moment of hope and humanity at a time when the country most needed it.

Initially there was some confusion, with people thinking they could take the animals home and look after them there. But 'sponsorship' – which is really what it was – wasn't a word that was in common use then, whereas 'adoption' was.

It was all meticulously organised. The list of potential candidates ran to 117. The most expensive was Patrick – he had been priced at 14/6 a week – followed by Punch at 14/-. Sally the Malayan bear came in at 2/-. Bernard, a rhesus monkey, was 9d, crowned cranes were 5/- for eight. An aviary of mixed parakeets cost 1/6d. Peter the capybara was also 1/6d. Faith, the first of Patrick's wives, had given birth to three healthy cubs – the zoo's first – early in August and they were available for adoption at 1/- a week each. As far as was possible, the weekly charge accurately reflected the expense of feeding each animal.

Jimmy, our youngest chimp, was the first to go – only to be expected, as he was such a favourite; an anonymous benefactor offered to adopt him for six months. As for the new lion cubs, born on 8 August 1939, they could each have been adopted several times over. Other choices were more surprising: the cane rat, for example – a shy nocturnal creature who was hardly ever seen – was oversubscribed. He had been 'won' by Mr Partington of Upton, who adopted him for seven weeks – others had to take their turn.

But there were still many animals whose names remained unticked, and plenty who had only been adopted for a week or two. A small boy at boarding school wrote asking to adopt one of the lion cubs for the duration of the war. When Dad replied explaining just how much it would cost – because cubs quickly grow up to be lions – the boy wrote back apologising, saying that he couldn't go ahead until he'd been home for Christmas, as he wasn't sure how much he had in his money box.

Above all, nobody knew how long the war would last, or when – or how – it would end.

It was a time of such uncertainty, and there were so many other concerns on people's minds, that the fate of zoo animals would have been understandably low in their list of priorities. So month after month, my father would remind readers of *Zoo News* – and no doubt place notices anywhere else he could think of – that without their financial help, however minimal, there wouldn't be a zoo, and without the zoo, the animals wouldn't survive.

The most important adoption – or at least the one which would have the longest-lasting effect – was Punch's. Miss Tomkyns Grafton, who lived near Windermere in the Lake District, had read about Miss Holt's generous donation of 400 birds and decided to visit the zoo to see them for herself. So on her return from a holiday in north Wales, she broke her journey and came to Upton. She later claimed that she had immediately developed an affinity with Punch. I know how she felt. In spite of his stubbornness, and having killed the peacock and a fox, there was something loveable about dear old Punch. She adopted him for four weeks, but the four weeks eventually lasted till the end of the war. In fact well beyond.

Although adopters couldn't take the animals home, they had visiting rights and the animals often benefited in a practical way by being given extra food or treats by their 'guardians'. The usual warning 'do not feed the animals' no longer applied. One lady, who had adopted Sally, would bring her almost-empty golden syrup tins. Unlike tin cans, the inner rim was smooth, so the lid could be prised up and replaced, and it would do no damage. Malayan bears are honey-eaters in the wild, and have extra-long tongues in order to reach honeycombs in crevices of tree trunks. As this lady had anticipated, the green and silver Tate & Lyle tins, with their trademark roaring lion, still had enough golden syrup clinging to the insides to be of interest. As soon as other visitors saw what Sally could achieve with her tongue, golden syrup tins became the new treat, so nobody was left out.

Charlie, our widower penguin, was visited every day by Miss Joan Walker, a local resident, who not only adopted him for the duration of the war at a cost of 1/6d a week, but brought him fresh herrings. And if anyone thinks that birds don't recognise humans, they should have seen him when she walked towards his pen.

My father's adopt-an-animal scheme was eventually copied by all other zoos in Britain, and subsequently by zoos across the world, and not only for the duration of the war. Adoption and sponsorship are now part of every zoo's vocabulary, and not only zoos. Endangered species across the world are helped by adoption. It is a legacy my father could be justly proud of.

Like many other children of my age, I had expected bombs to drop out of the sky the day war was declared. And I'm ashamed to say I was a bit disappointed when they didn't. Barrage balloons – designed to force enemy planes to go higher, where ack-ack guns could fire on them – went up fairly swiftly. Apart from that, though, nothing seemed to happen. It was a period that became known as the Phoney War.

For me, it began to become real when the news came through of the sinking of HMS *Courageous,* the aircraft carrier that Dad and I had seen at Portland during the review of the fleet. It was the first British warship to be lost at sea.

Apart from the surreal landscape of silver barrage balloons floating above the ground, tethered to the earth by metal cables, the only change I noticed were the evacuees. You'd hear children talking in the street or at the bus stop and know instantly that they didn't come from the local area because of their strong Liverpool accents. A few months later, shortly before Holland was invaded by Germany, two Dutch girls called Ella and Anna started at my school. They were staying with friends who had a daughter in my class.

On 25 September the zoo had its largest-ever group visit when Dad gave free entry to over a thousand evacuees, brought by their teachers. It was a Monday, so I was at school and didn't see them, but I heard all about it when I got home. They were mainly from poor areas of Liverpool, Dad said, and for most of them this was their first-ever visit to a zoo. I would have loved to have been there. Most of these children had never seen live wild animals before, only photographs – and in those days that would have meant black and white. Dad said that they were open-eyed with wonder, though not open-mouthed, as they never stopped talking.

Subsequent to this, he decided to build on the zoo's educational aspect. For some time there had been discounted rates for parties of cubs and brownies, as well as scouts and girl guides, but from now on the cheap rate of 2d would be extended to any child on any weekday, as long as there were adequate teachers to supervise.

Children weren't the only evacuees. Soon after his adoption scheme had been announced, Dad got a phone call from Mr Herbert Whitley of Paignton Zoo in Devon. The zoo had started life during the First World War as Mr Whitley's private collection in the grounds of his house, and was much appreciated locally and by holidaymakers, but because of the issue about 'entertainment tax', he had closed it to the public in

1937. Now the whole coastline – particularly where there were sandy beaches, like Paignton – was vulnerable to invasion and Mr Whitley believed his animals were under threat. Could Mr Mottershead look after some of them? He could. They would not be with us permanently, Dad explained, they were simply evacuees. On offer were four tahrs (a kind of mountain goat), three leopards, a binturong (also known as bearcats), a civet cat, a bush buck, a large puttynosed monkey, a large mona monkey, a griffon vulture, a buzzard and a porcupine.

Not long after, Dad had another call, this time from Mr Wilsden of Dudley Zoo. Again, this had started as a private collection by Lord Dudley in the grounds of Dudley Castle. I'd been there with Dad shortly after it opened and the enclosures were built on the same ditch/moat principles he now aspired to. It was small and, thanks to Lord Dudley's private fortune, well-funded. But Dudley was close to Birmingham – a centre of heavy industry, where, among other things, Spitfires and tanks were being built. Could Dad help? He could, and we welcomed a pair of American bison, a llama, a fallow deer, four coypu, five racoons, a Stanley crane, a Barbary ram, an otter and two wallabies. Needless to say, the candidates-for-adoption list was quickly growing longer.

The arrival of the new animals did not pass

without incident. Accommodation was in short supply and when three leopards arrived from Paignton – rather than the two my father was expecting – they were housed in adjoining cages. For nearly a week they took little notice of each other, so it was decided to let them run together, to allow the keeper to clean out the cage. When the sliding door between the cages was opened the young female walked through. Within seconds the male sprang at her. She struggled to get free, but he had such a strong hold that she never stood a chance. Immediately the keepers turned the hose on them, but to no avail. Then a smoke bomb was thrown, in another attempt to separate them. Finally, after fifteen minutes of being clamped in his jaw, she went limp and the male proceeded to drag her around the cage. It was obvious she was dead. When he was finally driven off, the keepers found that her neck had been broken at the base of her skull. But apart from teeth marks on her head, the body showed no signs of this horrifying killing. Later that year her unblemished skin was offered in a draw to raise money for the zoo. Two thousand tickets were sold – this included entry – which was a huge relief and kept the zoo going through the following winter.

Another skin that later raised money in the same way was that of the habitual escaper, Sammy the Malayan bear. The winter of

1940 was long and cold and after a day of non-stop blizzard, snow had drifted into the bears' ditch. Sammy, who although he came from a tropical climate, never seemed to worry about the cold, was intrigued by this new white world. Paw prints going across the drift and over the wall showed that he had known exactly what to do. Once out, he made his way to the house.

Marjorie was in the hall, waiting for her boyfriend to come and take her to the pictures. When she heard a noise at the door she thought it was Frank. She put out the hall light, turned the handle and in walked Sammy. Dad and Mum heard her scream from upstairs and both rushed down. By then Sammy was exploring, climbing on the counter and generally looking around, utterly unconcerned. Dad handed Marjorie a bag of sweets. They would get his attention, he assured her, and give him time to get a travelling crate in place, but he told her to take no chances. He'd be back, he said, in very short order. By the time Frank turned up, the crisis seemed to be over. Sammy was sitting back on his haunches while Marjorie was feeding him the sweets one by one. But then the sweets ran out and Sammy wasn't happy and turned his attention to the furniture. Chairs and tables went flying, then he started clawing at the oak panelling – you can still see the marks today. The noise of the crate being delivered to the front door was enough to frighten him. He climbed on the counter and, from there, threw himself through the stained-glass section of the mullioned window, landing in the snow unhurt but very angry. Looking at it now, you wonder why he would have done it. But the coloured panels are only at the top, whereas the bottom half is plain.

Dad got his gun and followed Sammy's paw prints, which wasn't difficult in the snow.

'When he got to the top of the drive,' Dad said, 'I had to make a choice. If he turned left – where we caught him the last time – I'd have carried on with the chase. If he turned right, towards the main road, I knew I'd have to shoot him.' Sammy turned right.

Dad's need to take on new keepers to replace the boys was now even more imperative. I can find no trace of the original advertisement he placed, but in November's edition of *Zoo News* he outlined the duties of a keeper much better than I could at this distance of time.

First there is the cleaning of cages which is of primary importance and this is done each day. Then the animals must have their meals attended to and in most cases this has to be prepared, care must be taken to give variety and prevent the animals from becoming food sick.

Very few of the animals need grooming but care has to be taken to see that they are given facilities to clean themselves.

Keeping the animals warm and protected from the weather is of vital importance and entails working in the wet and wind. There are very few animals or birds that like wind. All try to avoid it at all cost.

Utensils have to be well cleaned and when sickness comes, as it often does even in the best regulated zoo, the animal has to be nursed according to its special requirements; it is not uncommon to sit up all night tending it.

The chief thing which turns most youths and girls away from this career is the long hours. Although the actual hours are somewhat similar to other vocations the keeper has to be on duty, that is, to stay within call for 24 hours each day. He of course gets his time off, when he usually leaves the zoo, for then only is he free from a possible call. Nevertheless to those who love animals, etc. and take an interest in their work it can be called a pleasant and enjoyable occupation.

The wage offered was 7/6 a week, and the day started at 7 a.m. Three hundred girls applied, and by the end of February, six had been accepted and were in their posts. They came from as far away as London and Manchester. One was a typist, another a nurse. None of them had any experience, so Dad

217

decided to provide a crash course in biology and zoology. In the December edition of *Zoo News* he had asked for donations towards a microscope and was given one within twenty-four hours.

I decided to go along to one of the lectures. To my mind, it wasn't a great success – the girls were too busy flicking through *Picture-goer* and buffing their nails. I never felt comfortable with them – they were all so smartly dressed compared to me and were obviously 'women of the world'. When the lecturer announced that 'the main purpose in life is to reproduce', they didn't turn a hair. I was slightly shocked.

Although the British government would rather have been wrong, the war didn't catch them unawares. Although there had been no conscription since the Great War, as it was then called, in May 1939 there had been a call-up of single men between the ages of twenty and twenty-two for six months c basic training. These were known as militi men, to distinguish them from regular s diers, and would be the first troops to onto war alert.

Poison gas had been used by Germai the trenches in 1914–18, so there w; reason to suppose that it wouldn't b∈ c this time and gas masks had alread ci issued. We had even had a dummy N school – an entire lesson conducted with this breathing apparatus clamped over our heads. We were supposed to practise using them for ten minutes every day, but they were so uncomfortable that hardly anyone did, at least not among my friends.

The masks were stored in a cardboard box with strings attached, so you could carry it over your shoulder. There was even a packet of chewing gum in the box, but what that was for, I can't imagine – perhaps to keep you calm. You had to carry it with you all the time, and the gas-mask drill – which we had every day – involved putting it on and breathing through it for five minutes. We also had air-raid drills, though not so regularly. When the siren sounded we would march in a crocodile across the road and down into the nearest shelter, which was next to the Roman walls. The sides and roof were made of corrugated iron and it was banked up with earth outside. Inside there were wooden benches. I can only remember a few sirens being sounded during school hours, as most air raids happened at night, by which time I was back at home.

The gas masks were very cumbersome and uncomfortable to wear, but we were so terrified of gas attacks that we never went anywhere without them. The air-raid drills continued and we helped put sticky tape across the windows so that, in the case of a blast, we didn't get cut by flying glass.

Although Chester itself wasn't considered a target, it was on the direct flight path to the Liverpool docks, through which 80 per cent of the country's food would come over the next six years. Cutting this umbilical cord was a top priority for Germany. Keeping it intact was ours. Without it, we literally couldn't survive.

Blackout blinds were soon up everywhere. Car headlamps and bike dynamos had to be masked, leaving just a narrow slit of light to see by. There were no street lamps and torches had to be kept very low. Nothing could help the bombers locate where they might be. You learned to see by the moon, but moonlit nights were also when raids would be at their worst. When the sky was cloudy, or there was nothing more than a crescent moon, it could be terribly dangerous, particularly on a bike. The worst obstacles were the emergency standpipes that had been put up everywhere (known as EWS) to provide water to hoses to put out fires. Although marked with luminous paint, they were lethal in the dark, and you'd hear people bumping into them and using what Granny would call 'choice language'. Occasionally a cheery bobby would take pity on me and accompany me as far as the lodge.

When it came to Oakfield, I don't know how we would have coped if we'd had a make blackout blinds for every window in the house. Luckily, although there had been no curtains when we arrived, there were navy-blue roller blinds made of a thick waxy material, and they were still there. As they didn't quite extend to the full width of the windows, Mum and I painted stripes of black paint down each side. And just as we'd done at school, I criss-crossed the windows with sticky tape.

With all the evacuees – many of them large – the zoo was now definitely overcrowded. Miss Johnson, a member of the council who lived in the Wirral, bought an adjoining field, giving the zoo the option to buy it later, which it did. This was used for non-danger-ous animals, like the bison, the llama and the white donkeys. Although the llama was happy to stay where he was, the bison were always getting out and would regularly be found grazing on the front lawn at night. The donkeys did too, though they at least were easy to spot. But with the bison, if you came home after dark, you'd have to listen out for their breathing and hope to skirt around them. On nights without a moon this was tricky.

The bison liked to wander in the direction of Mr Cheers's farm, where the bull, Fer-nand, attempted to mate with one of the cows. Mr Cheers was enraged when he found this had happened and threatened to sue if his cow gave birth to a hybrid. But, as Dad pointed out, any such offspring would in fact be incredibly valuable.

Faith's cubs – named Coral, Cordelia and Cassandra – the first to be born in the zoo, were now growing big and strong and a hole had been made in her private den so that the cubs had access to the field outside, where they could play. Even though she couldn't go with them, she was still very much in charge, and the moment she made a noise, they would come skittering back in.

One evening I was out for a walk with Marjorie and Jet, and we were watching the cubs having fun jumping over some old tyres in the field when I spotted a man raising a shotgun, apparently taking aim.

I yelled out, 'Put that down!' Until that moment, he hadn't seen us. As he turned, I ran towards him, Jet racing by my side shouting, 'What do you think you're doing

'Out shooting rabbits,' he said.

'Well, those animals belong to the whose land, incidentally, you're trespa on.'

'I thought they were hares,' he said.

'Well they're not. They're lions.'

And at this, he beat a hasty retrea

We realised that, sooner or l liberty the cubs had been given w to be curtailed. But the exercise for them and Dad decided to let it continue as long as they behaved themselves.

A few days after Christmas the keeper reported that one of the cubs was having difficulty squeezing in and out of the hole. A few days after that another returned covered in blood. Then the second one, also covered in blood and barely able to squeeze through the hole. There was no sign of the third. It was late afternoon, the sky was very low and it was extremely cold. I had just got back from school and was in the kitchen, talking with my mum, eating some bread and jam and warming my hands by the range, when Dad walked in.

'That's it,' he said, looking grim.

'What's it?' Mum asked.

'Faith's cubs – there could be trouble. I'd like to think they killed a rabbit, except there's too much blood.'

'What about a hare then?' I suggested, thinking of the man I'd seen.

'I'm going out to take a look,' he said, collecting his gun.

'Do you really need that, George?' Mum said.

'I'm taking no chances.'

'Wait for me, Dad. I'm coming with you.' But he had already gone.

I caught up with him as he was striding across the field where I'd seen the man shooting rabbits.

'The third one is still out,' he said. 'That's who we're looking for, so keep your eyes skinned.'

Jet was now racing ahead and when she reached the next field, she stopped and barked. Dad broke into a run, only slowing up when he reached the gate. He didn't go through and I soon caught up with him. There, not five yards away, were the remains of one of the piebald sheep that we'd been given a year or so previously. Beside him, a fat lion cub was licking her paws. She was so full that she made no attempt to move. Dad went over, picked her up by the scruff of her neck and marched off back to the zoo. That was the last of their liberty.

Charlie Collins had been born with curvature of the spine – what louts from the village would sometimes call a hunchback – and although Dad never admitted as much, I know he hoped Charlie would fail his medical. As far as Dad was concerned, Charlie was irreplaceable. He was by now an expert gardener and a first-class bricklayer (the lion house owed its existence entirely to him). He was also one of the nicest people you could ever hope to meet. Unfortunately for us, he was also a very good driver and, although he had failed the medical, by the middle of 1940, he was with RAF Transport Command, based in the Cotswolds, where the land, being both high and flat, was home to dozens of airfields. Charlie's job was to tow aircraft from one place to another. His patch was just north of Swindon in Wiltshire – the airfields at Blakehill Farm, Broadwell and Down Ampney. A plane could only move on its own when it was in the air, so if one was damaged – or had come down in the wrong place – a trailer known as a Queen Mary was used to transport it (so named because the Cunard liner the *Queen Mary* was then the longest in the world). Although planes were generally light, they were long, and moving them was a highly skilled job, especially along narrow country lanes. While the airfields in Lincolnshire, East Anglia and Kent were central to the Battle of Britain, these Cotswold airfields played an important role in Operation Overlord, otherwise known as D-Day.

At least it meant Charlie didn't have to go abroad, and he would spend every leave back in Upton, mowing the lawns and helping Granddad out in other ways. Granddad was now eighty-five and was still trying to do everything, and I think that's why Charlie always showed up, though it was often Dad who would commandeer him for jobs. At the end of the war he came back for good, probably for the same reason – because the zoo was his family. His wife and daughters also did stints over the years, in a variety of guises. Charlie retired in 1982, after forty-nine years of faithful service. He died on 2 September 1993, aged seventy-five, and I still miss him.

Another member of staff to leave that first spring of the war was Peter Falwasser, our aquarist. In the short time since it had opened, the aquarium had become one of the zoo's star attractions. In fact, at £1 week, it was the most pricey of any exhibit put up for adoption – though for that you did get hundreds of beautiful fish. Once I knew Peter was going, I did everything I could to persuade my parents that I should take over. I implored them. I could do it in the evenings and at weekends, I said.

'It's hard enough to get you to concentrate on your school work as it is. No.'

I remember my anger when I arrived home one evening to find my father sitting in the kitchen, his head in his hands. He looked up when he heard the door go and gave me a wan smile.

'Dad? What's wrong?'

It turned out that all the fish in one of the tropical tanks had died. The girl in charge had put in cold water. Just a mistake, he said. The mistake was in trusting them to people who knew nothing.

Unless they've had a fright or been badly hurt, young animals – like young children –

are fearless. Growing up where she did, Jet had no sense that she was surrounded by predators who might want to harm her. She had no fear of any of the smells that wafted through the zoo. Like any other dog, she spent much of her time sniffing, but as long as it was a smell she knew, she wasn't worried.

When Jet wasn't with me, her favourite occupation was looking for rats. For no apparent reason, her ears would prick up and she'd be off, and you'd see her tearing around, dashing into the undergrowth or a clump of azaleas, or barking at a corner of an old building – and you'd know what it was. When this happened, I'd always tell Dad because rats were a constant problem, as they were often the carriers of infection. Most animals in zoos don't die of old age, they die because they get ill. Treating them is always difficult and sometimes impossible, and prevention is always better than cure.

One evening I was doing my homework when Dad came in. He wanted to borrow Jet, he said, to go ratting. One of the girls had told him she'd seen one by a drain near the old blacksmith's shop – where Punch had been kept in the early days. Jet's ears were up and she was scampering around from side to side, looking up at Dad and giving her little yaps. Then they were off.

I only know what happened next from what

Dad told me later. They were going around the courtyard when suddenly Jet started barking and a rat ran out and headed straight for the lion house. Before Dad knew it, Jet followed, squeezing herself under the lowest bar of Patrick's cage, which couldn't have been more than four inches off the ground. The rat escaped, but Jet wasn't quick enough and Patrick grabbed her in his mouth, but then – as if surprised at what had happened, Dad said – he dropped her. Dad immediately called for help, got Patrick away, then retrieved poor Jet. Her chest had been crushed and there were deep round holes where Patrick's teeth had penetrated.

I'd heard none of the commotion. No noise except for a few yaps, which I'd put down to Jet having found her quarry. Dad came into the kitchen holding Jet in his arms like a baby. I knew something terrible had happened when I saw his face. He stood at the door and just looked at me, and said, 'I'm sorry. It was Patrick.' I stood up and Dad came over and passed her across. She wasn't dead. She was still breathing, looking up at me with a bewildered expression in her eyes. Dad handed me the blanket from the cardboard box that she used as a bed and which was always by the range, and I wrapped it around her, sat down and just cradled her. Her breath was coming in short pants.

'She's dying, isn't she?' I said.

'Yes.'

'Is there nothing we can do?'

'Nothing.'

I sat there with her on my lap for about ten minutes. Her eyes would close and then open again, as if she was tired. She made no noise. I talked to her, like I'd talked to her so many times before. And then she was gone. It was the first time I'd watched someone I loved die. It brought home to me the difference between the body and the spirit. Once the spirit has left, there is no more life. The body that I put in the box, wrapped in her old blanket, wasn't Jet anymore.

When you live in a zoo you get used to animals dying. You have to. But the next morning Dad went out early and dug a grave under a laurel bush. He found stones to edge it with, then a large flat piece of sandstone to mark the place, and he carved her name on it. He felt responsible. He knew what Jet had meant to me. She wasn't a zoo animal who I'd been advised to keep my distance from. She was a pet. An ordinary, everyday pet. I mourned for her and put fresh flowers on her grave for many years. That morning, as I walked away, my eyes blurred with tears, I decided that I hated lions and made up my mind that I would never have anything to do with them again.

Chapter 9

On 21 June 1940 I celebrated my fourteenth birthday, though 'celebrated' is probably not the right word.

On the same day a Norwegian ship, the *Randsfjord*, was torpedoed and sunk by a German U-boat. It was carrying ammunition and thirty-three aircraft and was headed for Liverpool.

The British steam tanker *San Fernando* was also torpedoed and sunk by a U-boat. It was carrying crude oil and fuel oil and was also headed for Liverpool.

The day before Vichy and Lyons were captured by the Germans.

A week before that (14 June) Paris had fallen.

Two weeks before that (between 27 May and 4 June) 338,000 troops of the British Expeditionary Force had been forced to retreat from Dunkirk, using every boat on the south coast they could lay their hands on, from paddle steamers to cabin cruisers. It was, said Churchill, when he addressed the House of Commons with his 'we shall fight them on the beaches' speech, 'a miracle of deliverance'. He had taken over as prime minister only two weeks before.

The day after my birthday France signed an armistice with Nazi Germany. From then on, the country would be split in two: the north would be occupied by Germany, the south administered by an 'independent' government in Vichy, headed by General Pétain, a national hero of the First World War.

Until now German planes hadn't had the range to bomb Liverpool – the main reason Paignton and Dudley zoos had sent their animals to us. Now, with every airport in northern Europe at the Luftwaffe's disposal, the *blitzkrieg* could start – and I was terrified.

Everything that Hitler said he would do, he did do. Czechoslovakia was invaded. Poland was invaded. Denmark was invaded. Norway was invaded. Holland was invaded. Belgium was invaded. And now France. Everything that we were doing, all the preparations that were being made, meant we would be next. Because he had said so.

'Don't forget, June, that Britain is an island,' my father said. 'The Germans can't just stroll across the border like they've done everywhere else because there's a sea in the way.' But I knew that the sea wasn't very wide. Even small boats had managed to get there and back when they'd brought our stranded troops back from Dunkirk.

'You're to stop worrying, do you hear? Just

concentrate on your school work. Don't forget, we've got Mr Churchill in the driving seat now. And I tell you what, if the Germans do come, we'll shoot them one by one and drop them down the well. They'll never find them and we'll just say we don't know anything about it.'

'I'd rather feed them to the lions.'

'Ah, but then there might be some evidence left.'

But I *was* worried. Sick with worry. So I joined the Girls Training Corps and did my bit by learning Morse code and first aid. And when the summer holidays started I took over at the aquarium. After all, as I reminded my parents, I was the same age as Mew had been when she became keeper.

And then, on 28 August 1940, the Liverpool Blitz began, and the assault continued for three nights without let-up. No one had known what to expect, as the London Blitz didn't start till ten days later. Over the next three months there were fifty raids. Some lasted no time at all. Others went on all night, with hundreds of bombers flying over the house destined for the docks at Liverpool and Birkenhead.

It soon became clear that the vibrations of the bombs had taken their toll and the tanks in the aquarium started leaking. There was nothing for it but to empty them. The cold-water fish were put back in the ponds, where many of them had come from originally. The tropical fish just died. They weren't even big enough to be fed to Pelly or Charlie. I remember feeling glad that Peter wasn't there to witness what had happened to all his work. I consoled myself with the thought that when he came back it would all be rebuilt better than before. He never came back. He was killed in north Africa in 1943, during the siege of Tobruk, fighting Rommel. But he had already given me his greatest gift: his knowledge and love of fish, for which I will be eternally grateful.

Now that the aquarium was empty, it became our air-raid shelter and, during those long nights, that's where we would go. There was no radio reception in the cellar, so we just had Dad's gramophone, but he would play the same old records over and over again. Boredom may not kill you, but it is very, very tiring. When it was time to go to sleep – or try to – I would lie on my camp bed, remembering those winter evenings with Charlie and Nippy, Sam and Billy, and what fun they had been. While Mum and Dad stayed in the sitting room – the old housekeeper's room – I'd sneak out and join the staff in the kitchen. Mew, Maud, Marjorie and the boys would all be crowded around the range, and there'd be Rob Rob taking chunks out of the chairs, and Jacky perched on the dresser, and they'd be playing games: charades, consequences, murder, quizzes and dares. One of the dares was to go outside in the dark and walk around the house, but hardly anyone did, because they got scared. If they were scared then, imagine what they'd be like now...

We soon gave up going to the aquarium. Everyone would rather risk it and sleep in their own beds. As for the cellar, it became a dumping place for 'things that might come in useful one day'.

Fire was Dad's greatest fear, much more so than a direct hit, which, he said, would be extremely unlikely. As for the danger of animals escaping, the instructions were 'shoot to kill'.

None of the fire guards from the village were prepared to patrol the zoo, as they were too frightened of the animals getting out, so I did it. Officially I was too young – women had to be between twenty and forty-five, and I wouldn't turn twenty until 1946, by which time the war had been over for a year – but with things as they were, we all had to do our share.

The instructions were in a booklet hanging on a hook near the phone.

The duty of a Fire Guard is to take turns in watching for the fall of fire bombs; to warn the neighbourhood when they fall in the area for which he is responsible; to help promptly to con-

234

trol them and thus to prevent small fires from becoming big fires; and to fit himself by training to perform the work efficiently.

It is work which sometimes requires courage and endurance; it involves the sacrifice of time that can sometimes be ill spared, and often entails a great deal of tedious waiting and watching; but it is work which must be done if the homes and industries of our Nation are to be saved.

Given the fact that no one from outside the zoo was prepared to do it, my age was glossed over, but to qualify, I first had to do a course. I learnt to use the stirrup pump – which had a long hose to stop you having to get too close to the fire – and to crawl through a room filled with smoke to rescue people and do first aid.

Because of our special circumstances, we'd be given an early warning of any impending raid by telephone, so someone would always have to answer it. Raid or not, the last thing we'd do every night was to check the animals were secure, as you never knew when one would come, and the phone could ring when you were least expecting it. The main phone had always been in the office, with an extension in the kitchen. Once the war started, another extension had been put on the landing at the top of the stairs, so everyone could get to it. The noise when bombers flew over the house was terrible, and everything rattled and shook. In spite of the blinds, you could see the beams of the searchlights criss-crossing the darkness, scanning the sky for Heinkels, to show them up so the gunners could bring them down before they reached the docks. Then would come the glow of Liverpool or Birkenhead burning. On their return journey, the planes made a different sound, as by then they were lighter, having dropped their bombs.

If it wasn't my turn for fire-watching, I'd be there listening to the whine of the siren, and then the throb of the bombers coming over and the rattling staccato of the ack-ack batteries that were just down the road on Acres Lane. We were close enough to hear the command 'Fire!' You could hear the shells exploding and the sound of shrapnel falling, like a hail of pebbles thrown onto a hundred tin roofs.

The coypu that had arrived from Dudley Zoo became the zoo's only casualty when a piece of shrapnel entered his neck. He was in a pen in the orchard and death must have been instant, as when they inspected his body, they found a chunk of uneaten bread between his teeth. Worst of all, Granddad's beautiful conservatory was so badly damaged by shrapnel and blasts that it was beyond repair. As it turned out, more damage was done by our own guns than by the enemy's.

I never had to put my fire-fighting skills into practice, as no incendiaries landed in the zoo, although five stick bombs fell on the Davies' farm and five cows were scorched. The noise didn't seem to worry the animals at all. If you went into the lion house during a raid – which I sometimes did on fire-watch duty – you would hear Patrick snoring and, if the cubs were awake, they'd show no signs of anxiety at all, but would be getting up to their latest trick of squeezing under the floorboards. The only animals that did seem a bit scared were the piebald sheep, who would run and stand close to Ferdinand the bison, as if they had explicit trust in his protective bulk.

In the ten years since the zoo had opened, it had never been closed, not even for Christmas. The Luftwaffe paid no attention to Christmas either, and over three days – 20–22 December – 365 people were killed in Liverpool, many of them in air-raid shelters. Nowhere was safe. In October we'd had news that Uncle Billy's step-daughter had been killed when she was out looking after a lamb, up on the farm in Westmorland. A bomb had exploded in the next field and she was blown sky high. Why? There was nothing up there except fells and crags.

'Could it have been an accident?' I asked my father. We were in the kitchen. Mum was upset and had gone upstairs.

'You could call it that,' Dad said. 'They were probably on their way back from a raid and had a bomb they hadn't dropped and wanted to lighten the load. I imagine the fells look deserted from up there. They might have thought it was better than dropping it on a town.'

Just before Christmas 1940 I was given a puppy by a friend of my dad's – in compensation, really, for what had happened to Jet. He was another terrier – small but not tiny, as Jet had been – a Sealyham with a shaggy white coat. He had a way of looking at you with his head on one side and I decided to call him Peter, in memory of Peter the capybara, who had died the previous spring. Peter the puppy was about six months old when three lion cubs arrived at the zoo who were about the same age. We always gave cubs from one litter names beginning with the same letter. So these were christened Valentine, Valerie and Victor. They had been given to the zoo by David Rosaire – one of the Rosaire family, famous animal trainers in Britain at the time. No sooner had they arrived than Valerie left to take up her role as a regimental mascot. Then, a week or so later, Valentine injured himself so badly when dashing across his cage that he had to be put to sleep.

Victor was inconsolable. In less than two

weeks he had lost his sister and his brother. And not long before that his mother, presumably. He cried piteously and it was while the keeper was trying to comfort him that Peter came up, inquisitive as always, his head cocked on one side. We decided to introduce them. At first Victor was suspicious, but Peter was oblivious and took no notice and when he started licking him, the lion cub allowed him to do it. The following day Peter arrived at Victor's cage without any prompting. So the keeper let him in and, after a little while, they started playing. When the time came for them to separate, the keeper said, it was obvious that neither of them wanted playtime to end. Victor was soon crying again, so Peter was allowed to go in with him the next morning.

Until then, I had known nothing of this. Perhaps people thought I would be upset, after what had happened to Jet. And I *was* worried. I grew up in a zoo. I know that wild animals are always wild animals, however cuddly they might look, and can turn on you at any time. It's true that Peter and Victor were the same age and at roughly the same level of development: learning through play. And there lay the problem, as far as I was concerned: what was Peter going to learn? That lions were safe? I didn't want that. But that third morning they were put together was a Saturday and I was home from school. Peter was my dog and I wasn't happy about him being with Victor, but I said, 'All right. Just one last time.'

At lunchtime I went to the lion house to fetch Peter to go for a walk and saw him and Victor playing together. I looked at them, and my heart melted. They were obviously so happy. I thought of Miss Russell Allen and the word she used to use: adorable. And they were completely adorable.

Peter and I had our walk, but no sooner were we back than he scampered across the courtyard to be with Victor, standing expectantly at the gate waiting to be let in. What was I to do? Nothing. It was like a passionate love affair and Peter moved in. He literally set up his permanent quarters with Victor, and from then on they shared everything, sleeping together, feeding together, all in perfect harmony.

Every day Peter would come out for a stretch and a bit of running around, and occasionally he'd pop back into the kitchen and settle down in his box by the fire. But it was never for long, and if anyone said the word 'Victor', up his ears would go, his tail would wag and he'd be off. As for Victor, he was as happy with the setup as Peter was.

Visitors were amazed. There was a lion – growing bigger by the week – with a very small dog pulling his ears and biting his lips, and Victor was letting it happen. And when

Peter came in, muddy after a run around the fields, it would be Victor who licked him clean. Dad, of course, was delighted, as was the press. But I was becoming increasingly worried.

'So when is this going to stop?' I asked.

'When the time comes for Victor to be a father, perhaps then, but that won't be for another three years or so.'

'Yes, but...'

'But nothing.'

The friendship of a lion and a dog was a crowd-pleaser. Nothing more to be said.

Of the six girls who'd joined the zoo early in 1940, only one was left. The others had decided that the life didn't suit them after all. Either that or Dad had decided they didn't suit the life. Anyway, being in uniform was far more glamorous than wearing dirty overalls and mucking out animal cages. The one who stayed was Barbara Wright, a really nice girl who was a lion keeper. She left the zoo when she turned eighteen and got her call-up papers and joined the land army. But as soon as the war was over, she came straight back.

To replace the girls, we had a boy called Henry of about my age, who hadn't stayed on at school and was still too young to be called up, but he would be soon. And when he went, we would just get another. Marjorie would help out when needed, and so would

Mum if things got desperate. But that winter it was just Dad, Barbara, Henry and me. These were dark days in all senses of the word.

On 31 January 1942 the regular three-monthly meeting of the council was held. Since the outbreak of war, the chairman of the society had been Mr Grounsell, who worked in insurance in Liverpool as a shipping loss adjuster. Hardly anyone turned up. The accounts for the previous year were not good. In spite of the adoption scheme, the society had shown a further loss of £431. Under these circumstances, grave doubts were voiced as to whether the zoo could stay open. Most of those present said that this would be the last meeting they'd be able to attend due to war work. A resolution was put forward that the society be wound up, but without a quorum present, no official decision could be taken.

And there was another cloud hanging over Dad's head: since the beginning of the year, anyone up to the age of fifty-one was liable to be called up. My dad was forty-five. And while he had been badly wounded at the Somme, he was as fit as anyone, and in fact had more energy than many people half his age. He had no reason to think he might be granted exemption.

The next day Dad and Mr Grounsell made their decision. They would carry on by themselves for another month or so, to see what developed. It wasn't just sentiment. Three weeks earlier the Japanese had attacked the American fleet at Pearl Harbor, and the following day America had declared war on Germany. Until now Britain – with the Commonwealth countries alongside – had been fighting alone. Although on paper America had been neutral until this point, without the convoys of arms and food coming across the Atlantic, we wouldn't have had a hope. When the Americans had entered the war in 1918, it had proved to be the beginning of the end, and there was a feeling of optimism that it would the same this time. They had such huge resources, of materials and of men. As far as Dad and Mr Grounsell were concerned, it was grounds, anyway, for hope.

Once the decision was made, I was despatched to get Miss Russell Allen's signature on the document that Dad and Mr Grounsell had drawn up. During the First World War she and her sister Doris had worked with the First Aid Nursing Yeomanry, and she had decided to do her bit in this war as well. Now she was matron of a convalescent home outside Nantwich. The only way you could get there was by bus. I don't now remember how many changes I had to make, but it seemed to take forever. I had never made such a complicated journey on my own. I remember clutching the envelope tightly, knowing that it was important.

I finally got there sometime in the afternoon. I was there on urgent council business, I told them downstairs, which was what Dad had told me to say. I was directed up the main staircase and when Miss Russell Allen opened the door, I hardly recognised her. She had always been so glamorous and now here she was in a nurse's uniform.

That wasn't the last time I would have to make my way halfway across Cheshire to get Miss Russell Allen's signature, but while the journeys were just as long, it was never as big an ordeal as that first time. At least I knew where I was going and what to expect.

Over the next few months a pattern developed which would last for more than twenty years. Every Sunday Mr Grounsell would arrive at the zoo – he lived in Heswall, about ten miles north, on the opposite side of the Wirral peninsula to Birkenhead. After popping in to say hello to my mother, he and my dad would walk around the grounds, looking at the animals and inspecting the state of the pens and enclosures – which every week got worse – and then they'd come back to the library and talk 'policy'. After that Mr Grounsell would go back to his wife for Sunday lunch.

Dad and Mr Grounsell's belief that things would get better was proved right.

RAF Burtonwood had been in operation

since January 1940 as a servicing and storage centre, but in June 1942 it was transferred to the American Air Force and became the largest airfield in England. It was just north of Warrington, less than fifteen miles away, as the crow flies, and – if the wind was in the right direction – you could hear the roar of the engines being tested. It was huge; at the height of its operations there were 18,000 American servicemen stationed there, and a good many of them found their way to the zoo.

Chester had been a garrison town for over three hundred years and during the war it was the headquarters of Western Command. Since September 1939, Dad had given free entry to any member of the armed forces who came in uniform, but these dashing Americans quite took our breath away. Compared to the people we normally met, they were exotic. And it wasn't just their accents and the fact that they were so free with their chewing gum. The uniforms of even the regular GIs were made of better material than those of British officers. There were some who came in groups and who were there mainly to have fun and to forget about the war for a few hours, but others would take Dad to the side and talk to him about different species and breeding. I think their motives were probably no different, they were just more educated.

Although entrance was free for them, once inside the gates, the Americans would spend money, buying handfuls of postcards to send 'back home' and ordering up whatever they could at the café. They were enthusiastic about everything and it was infectious.

Sometimes they brought children with them – English children. How they found them, I have no idea. These days such a thing would look suspicious to some, but I suppose they were just missing their own kids and 'borrowed' whoever they thought would enjoy a day out.

The café was now a buffet where you served yourself. We continued to do salads – Granddad's output defying 'the Huns', as he liked to call them. There was also soup – homemade by Mum – and sandwiches, but instead of ham there was Spam, an insipid-looking luncheon meat. Mum still managed to do a bit of baking, but with dried eggs instead of fresh, and using lard instead of butter in the pastry for her pies.

Food was in short supply everywhere. Rationing had started in January 1940, so by then we'd had two years of it. Compared to people who lived in cities we were lucky, as most people we knew kept chickens and they'd bring us eggs, though the official ration was only one per week.

Against that was the constant pilfering of fruit from the orchard. This ranged from visitors just wandering through and deciding they quite fancied a bite, without thinking what they were doing, to gangs of youths coming in through the hedge at night, who would take away boxes full of apples.

Not far from the zoo – half a mile at most, the other side of the bypass – was the Dale Barracks, headquarters of the Cheshire Regiment and an important training centre for machine-gunners from across the country. Every morning the soldiers would run in full battledress down the Caughall Road, and the sergeant had taken to shouting 'Halt!' and 'Fall Out!' the moment they arrived at our gates, at which point they would all pour into the orchard and help themselves. When Mum discovered what was happening, she went absolutely crazy and telephoned their commanding officer.

'Do you realise,' she said, 'that your soldiers are stealing our staple food?'

'They're just young men,' he said, 'scrumping a few apples.'

'You can call it what you like,' she retorted. 'Where I come from we call it theft.'

It didn't happen again.

When American servicemen visited the zoo, they would sometimes bring their own food to supplement what Mum could offer. We would watch them open these tins and packets with wonder. They even had chocolate!

From April 1942, ordinary people could no longer buy petrol for their cars. It had been the first thing to be rationed in September 1939. Now it was only for reserve occupations. This must have given the zoo a boost. Trains and buses were still running and the fine weather that Easter and Whitsun saw takings running at 1939 levels.

By this time, although we had grown used to the war and its privations, it had become a little more bearable because everyone was in the same boat. For young people, there wasn't much to do, except go to the pictures. The seaside was out of bounds – every beach was patrolled, covered with rolls of barbed wire, and sand dunes were dotted with pillboxes manned by gunners. So what about a day at the zoo? Plenty of opportunities for flirting and catching the eye of some young man in uniform, perhaps even an American!

The other great boost was when Kay and the elephants arrived. They had been stranded in England since the outbreak of war, having been employed by Doorlay's Tropical Experience Revue. Curt Doorlay was an English-born theatrical impresario whose revues mixed circus and variety acts and mainly toured in Europe and South America, but in the summer of 1939 they had been in England. The rest of the troupe had managed to get out and find their way to South America, but having two elephants in tow didn't make life easy for Kay. He had contacted the Forestry Commission to get work moving logs – which was traditionally what elephants did in Ceylon. But they turned him down; they didn't have the facilities, they said. Since then, he had taken any job he could find, but had now run out of steam and ideas and money.

My father claimed that he had been written to by several children, following articles in the press saying that these two elephants might have to be destroyed if a home couldn't be found for them. These children, he said, promised to give him their pocket money if Chester Zoo would give them a home. I don't know if that's true – my father didn't allow the truth to get in the way of a good story. What I do know is that he and I went down by train to Northampton and saw these two elephants and their 'mahout', Khanadas Karunadasa, in an old locomotive shed near the station. He and his elephants were from Ceylon, but his name proved so unpronounceable that we always called him Kay (except for the locals in the Wheatsheaf in Upton, who – I discovered years later – called him Harry).

Molly was then about twenty, and Mannikin eight, and Dad decided he would take them. They would be a definite 'attraction' and would soon start earning their keep by giving rides. (In 1943 Molly earned the zoo

£200.) As for their food, at least they weren't carnivores – they lived on leaves, grass and hay in the wild. The agreement with Curt Doorlay's agent was that Dad would take them for the duration of the war and for one season after, in order to recoup some of the zoo's costs.

The first problem was where to house them. The wire mesh surrounding the griffon vultures' cage, sited since the beginning above the main entrance to the courtyard, had recently disintegrated. As there had been no money to mend it, they had been moved elsewhere.

This entrance – topped by a carved stone archway – was where the coaches would originally have come in, and was sufficiently high to allow for the grooms and footmen not to knock their heads. It would be tall enough, Dad decided, to serve as a structure which could be extended sufficiently to shelter the elephants, at least till something more permanent could be built.

Their arrival, he decided, would be celebrated with appropriate razzmatazz. No prize for guessing who would be at the station to greet them. But at least I wouldn't be alone; my cousin George, Uncle Charlie's youngest – the only one who'd really been interested in animals, and who was staying with us for the Easter holidays – would be coming with me.

Kay, Molly and Mannikin arrived in

Chester by train. But we'd have to walk from the station. My job – and George's – was just to march in front of them. At school I had always tried to play down my involvement with the zoo, but elephants coming to Chester wasn't something you could be quiet about for very long and I knew that among the crowds watching from the pavement would be some of my class. I could have died from embarrassment.

Our route lay along the main road – the old Roman road – which I would cycle on every day to get to school. From time to time I would stop and look round, just to check if they were following. The moment I stopped, they stopped. I had met Kay once before, in Northampton, but until that afternoon I hadn't really understood the nature of his relationship with the elephants. It was simply incredible – and became more incredible the better I got to know him. Kay was then about twenty-five and he had been with Molly since he was a little boy and she was a baby. There wasn't a thing he didn't know about her or that she wouldn't do for him.

Soon the ordeal was over and we were safely back on familiar territory, and the elephants were put in the orchard to enjoy the wholesome goodness of the Cheshire grass. The first time I'd seen them had been in a warehouse, where the light hadn't been that good. Now I could see that they were in a really bad state. Their ears were misshapen from frostbite and Mannikin, in particular, was very weak.

He died two weeks after they arrived.

Chapter 10

I left school in July 1942, at the end of the summer term, shortly after my sixteenth birthday. With the future of the zoo still up in the air, Dad and Mum had decided I needed a contingency plan. As I had always loved doing Granny's hair, they'd arranged for me to start an apprenticeship at Nixon's in Market Square in Chester the following September.

In the meantime, Mew came back on leave. I'd seen her a few times over the past three years, when Mum and I had visited her in Paignton and then Pwllheli, north Wales. None of her postings were on active ships. HMS *Glendower* was a stone frigate, as they called shore establishments, and had been a Butlin's holiday camp – now the chalets were used to house sailors. As Mum and I weren't allowed on the base, we stayed in a hotel in Criccieth, eight miles along the coast, and Mew would come to see us there. Now she'd written to me, saying that she didn't want to be sucked into life at the zoo and had decided to spend her leave visiting Uncle Kit and Uncle Billy in Westmorland, and she wondered if I'd like to go with her.

This wasn't Hunger Hill Farm, where my mother had been born and brought up, between Haweswater and Shap, but a small village – more a hamlet really – called Firbank, by the River Lune, a mile or so west of Sedbergh. When my grandparents had moved there, Granny had travelled in a horse and cart, but Granddad had covered the twenty-five-mile journey on foot with the bull.

I'd last been there when I was about eight or nine. This time would be different, as my mother's parents were dead: Thomas Atkinson had passed away in 1936 and Hannah in 1938, both aged seventy-eight. After they died, Mum had come into a bit of money. With it she bought headstones for both her parents, who are buried in Firbank church, and a headstone for little Frankie, who's buried at Wybunbury, near Shavington. The rest of the money she spent on her daughters – probably through guilt, feeling that she didn't give us enough of her time. But it did mean that I could have a brand new bicycle, which changed my life. Not only did it mean I could cycle to school every weekday but at weekends I'd visit my friend Nancy Lloyd on her farm. It was a Raleigh, and black – I don't think other colours existed in those days – with a basket on the front that was just the right size for Jet. While she had always loved running alongside my old bike, the idea of being up in the air whizzing along, in a position of such superiority, became her idea of pure bliss. The moment I got back from school and had taken off my uniform, there she would be dancing around the bike which I'd left by the back door, looking up at me expectantly. She was too small to jump in by herself, but when I bent down to pick her up she was trembling with excitement. We never went far – mostly just around the grounds – but sometimes I'd ride a mile or so up the Caughall Road and back again.

Although about eight years had passed since I'd last been up to Westmorland, the farm had hardly changed: a square-looking house, built of rough stone painted white, with a small walled-in garden at the front, just high enough so that the animals couldn't get in and eat all the plants. Across the cobbled yard was the shippon – what they called the cowshed, where the milking was done. It still looked and smelled exactly as I'd remembered it. Behind it was the old stone barn, with a ladder going up to the hayloft. The kitchen was still dominated by a big black range, with the same pewter mugs hanging from the beams. Although there was a front room, it was hardly ever used and was always very cold, so the kitchen was where everyone congregated, including the two black-and-white sheepdogs, mother and daughter, whose names I can't now remember.

Leading off the kitchen on the north side was where meat carcasses would be hung and the butter churned. Each pat was stamped with the farm's mark before it went to market, so that people could tell where it came from.

In the cellar there were large earthenware jars, glazed on the inside. When Granny had been alive they'd held the wine she used to make every year from nettles, elderberries and damsons. My uncles didn't bother with that anymore – perhaps it was something only women did – but the cellar still had the same pungent smell as it had had when she was alive.

The bedroom where Mew and I slept was exactly as I remembered it: whitewashed walls, feather mattresses, eiderdowns and patchwork quilts. My granny had been a very good needlewoman and one of the few things Mum brought with her to Oakfield from Shavington was a framed needlepoint picture of a boy carrying a brace of grouse, done by Granny when she was a girl. It was always said that she'd come from a 'good' family, which was why there had been money available for Dad to borrow to buy Oakfield and to pay for Muriel's and my education at the convent.

The outdoor privy, with its diamond-shaped peephole to let in some light, was the same and there was still no electricity, though Uncle Kit showed me how he'd made a generator, using the force of the beck as it tumbled down the steep hillside, to charge batteries, so they could listen to the radio. The river also offered up salmon, from time to time, he said, when they made their way up the Lune from the sea to spawn, but I wasn't to breathe a word, as they were owned by Lord Lowther, the Earl of Lonsdale, 'like everything else round here'.

The only thing that had changed was the people. Now it was just Uncle Kit and Uncle Billy and his wife, who had come as their housekeeper when Granny died. Although the two brothers looked very similar – thin and muscular because they were always working, and you'd never see either of them without a shirt and a waistcoat – they were very different in character. Uncle Kit was the extrovert, while Uncle Billy said nothing much at all. The youngest of Mum's brothers, who they called Bob, wasn't there, as he'd emigrated to New Zealand in 1938.

Uncle Robert was perhaps my favourite of Mum's three brothers. He would send me postcards – the first was from the Pitcairn Islands, which he'd sent me on the voyage out. I would always write back, telling him what was happening at the zoo, so we developed quite a correspondence. When he

257

arrived in New Zealand he bought a motor-cycle and travelled round the country, working with a group of sheep-shearers, something he would have been able to do in his sleep. But once war broke out he joined New Zealand's Expeditionary Force, the 21st Infantry Battalion. Before he left he wed a girl from Auckland. Even then the postcards didn't stop and he'd send me one from everywhere he went: from Palestine, from Egypt and Tunisia. I kept them all.

By 1943 the Kiwis were in Italy, crossing river after river, moving north after invading Sicily. The tide had begun to turn in the Allies' favour when the German army had failed to take Stalingrad, but progress up through Italy was slow. Uncle Robert died in the Battle of the River Sangro on 28 November 1943. We only found out that he'd been killed when one of the thin blue airmail letters of mine was returned unopened. One of the worst things I ever had to do in my life was to tell my mother.

He was thirty-six.

For those few days in the summer of 1942, Muriel and I ate better than we had for years: bacon and eggs, even roast lamb on Sunday. One morning we went for a walk and took the shortcut across the Lowgill Viaduct to Sedbergh. I remembered walking across that great span with eleven arches with Mum. In 1937 when we went after Granddad Atkinson died, we'd arrived by train from Chester and, after a number of changes, got off at Lowgill Halt. It was a long walk up to Bower's Farm, but nobody had come to pick us up or help us on the way back, which was hard, especially going back, as Granny had given Mum her sewing machine, which she had to carry. I remember following the railway track across the viaduct and being terrified that a train would come and that would be that.

Although I'd seen Muriel in Pwllheli, we'd not had time alone since she'd joined up in 1939 and, even then, we'd never really talked because she was nearly ten years older than me. But as you get older age differences become less important. And that morning we talked openly and honestly to each other, perhaps for the first time. When I asked if she missed the zoo, she hesitated. She missed the chimps, she said, but otherwise no, not really. She had hoped to be posted abroad, but the furthest she'd gone was Dunoon, on the west coast of Scotland. HMS *Ariel* was another stone frigate, and Muriel had worked there as a cook. She longed to travel and when the war was over she would, she said.

Mew had a sweetheart, a boy called Harry, who was Dutch. He'd managed to get out of Holland when the Germans moved in, escaped to England and joined the British Navy.

'Is Harry "the one", do you think?' I asked.

She laughed. 'I'm not sure such a person exists.'

'Well, I am.'

'That's because you're still young enough to be a romantic.'

In fact, having nowhere else to go, Harry came to stay with us when he was next on leave. He had a good sense of humour and I liked him. But after the war he went back to Holland and Muriel came back to the zoo. In the end, the chimps won.

Before we left Westmorland, I took my sketchpad and went up on the hill behind the farm, looking east over the Lune to Howfell, and drew a picture I would later turn into a watercolour. It was hard to imagine that a bomb had dropped here just two years before. Now the crater was a pond surrounded by grass and wild flowers: red and white campions, scabiouses, harebells and ox-eye daisies.

Nixon's was in a large basement off Northgate Street, under Taylor's garage, and they let me leave my bike there, not only when I was working downstairs but also in the evenings, when I went to the pictures or even dancing.

The salon was run by Beryl, a platinum-blonde. The décor was green and cream, with a beautiful patterned Turkish carpet on the floor and easy chairs for clients to sit on while they waited. Once their stylist was ready, they would go into their cubicle and a curtain would be drawn, so no one could see.

It could take up to five years to qualify as a hairdresser and I started from the bottom, sweeping up hair from the floor and shampooing. As I massaged scalps, I would think of how every animal enjoys being groomed or preened. This was no different really.

As well as working at Nixon's, I was still helping out at the zoo at weekends and on Wednesday afternoons, but every Friday, while the evenings were still light, I would cycle over to Nancy's. Mrs Lloyd was a widow and every Friday she went out to the pictures. She would leave us a huge salad and hard-boiled eggs, all fresh from the farm, plus lots of coffee brewing on the Aga. Nancy, her sister Margaret and I would play tennis on their lawn, where a court was marked out in white paint. It might not have been as good as a proper tennis court, but it was reasonably level and had a proper net. There were quite a gang of us who played – a girl cousin of the Lloyds', another farmer's daughter whose name I can't remember. If there was nobody else around to make up a four, then Jimmy, Nancy and Margaret's younger brother, would play, but he was only about nine. We always hoped to get one of the Charmley brothers – John or Richard – to make it more fun. Again they were farmer's sons who were never called up. There was always a selection of tennis rackets in the back porch, ranging from good ones to one we called 'the spoon', as that was its shape, which was only ever used as a last resort. If the weather was good we girls would cycle into the Wirral, beyond Neston, to Parkgate Baths, a huge outdoor swimming pool that was filled with salt water from the Dee Estuary.

I knew Nancy best because we were in the same class, but there was only a year and a half between her and her sister, so Nancy was nine months younger than me and Margaret was nine months older, and we were always together.

Their farm was in a village called Blacon, about three miles west of Upton, the other side of the railway line. We all had bicycles and in the summer we would cycle into north Wales, to Llangollen, and freewheel down the Horseshoe Pass. There was a beekeeper we'd met who kept hives on the moor and he'd sell us honey still on the comb. I can still remember the feeling of decadence as the honey dripped down my chin. On the moors there was a lake that was so tempting after the long pull up that one day we decided to throw off our clothes and go for a swim. I thought it would be freezing, but the sun had been out and it was lovely and warm. When we returned the next time it had been fenced off – perhaps someone had seen us.

We were all so fit in those days and we would race up the hills as if they were nothing. One day, towards the end of the war, there was a slope of purple heather, so springy and inviting that I cycled down it and jumped off, letting the bike career on, and it nearly ran into a prisoner of war and his girlfriend, who had been canoodling there. I don't know who was the more shocked!

One of the reasons I now had more freedom was that Kay had become a core part of the team. He worked wherever Dad needed him. Many animals – particularly lions – are frightened of elephants, and Kay did everything he could to eradicate the smell of Molly so he could work with them. To this end, he would cover himself with eau-de-cologne so liberally that the whole house would reek of it. Until then I had only associated perfume with rich, glamorous women. Not that Kay wasn't glamorous. He was, and also he owned such luxurious things – like a camera and a camel-hair overcoat – that I thought he must be very rich. Kay also caught the eye of Dorothy, one of the cashiers, and in 1943 they married and had a baby girl called Nathalie. Their 'flat' was above the kitchen, where the boys used to sleep before the war.

Within nine months of having decided to go it alone, Dad and Mr Grounsell were feeling optimistic that they had made the right decision. From May onwards, the number of visitors had grown steadily until August, which showed a 100 per cent improvement on 1939. Meanwhile takings from the café were up by 200 per cent. Granddad's fresh salads and Mum's homemade cakes and pastries were a great improvement on what was on offer elsewhere. Although the cages and pens were in a sorry state of repair, the range of animals had considerably enlarged since the outbreak of war. Molly was unquestionably a huge success. Queues of children waited patiently to climb up the steps and onto the howdah, and the moment they got off, they would rush back to join the queue again. Her great swaying figure, with Kay walking at her head, and her seated cargo of excited children had become one of our landmarks.

That summer the Korda brothers' film of *The Jungle Book* had its premiere in London. It was an overnight sensation – exactly what the war-weary public was looking for. It starred Sabu as Mowgli, a 'man-cub' reared by wolves in the Indian jungle. When it came to Chester, it was a publicity opportunity that was too good to miss, and Dad decided to rename Victor as Mowgli. The pretext was that Mowgli had been adopted by wolves, and Victor had been adopted by Peter. Peter was at the renaming ceremony, of course, and made a show of trying to drag Mowgli's huge bone away. More problematic had been finding someone to perform the naming. Dad had tried to find a starlet – he'd had success in the past getting pretty girls to name cubs – but Victor/Mowgli was a fully grown lion, or at least looked like one to most people, and no one well-known was prepared to risk it. Finally a game young reporter called Joan Hyland from the *Southport Journal* agreed. I remember that her whole body was shaking when she went into the pen. She was absolutely petrified, and with very good reason.

One Saturday afternoon, when the zoo was teeming with people, I was standing at the till taking money for teas when a man rushed in, in a great state of panic. A lion had got his overcoat, he said, and he demanded to see the head keeper. He said that a lion had stretched out its paw and grabbed it and he needed someone to go in and get it back. Of course it was a lie. The bars of the cage were about eight feet away from the spectators, so it was impossible. Later a woman came forward and said she'd seen this man climb over the first barrier, move aside a palm tree in a pot, and then begin flipping his coat against the bars, trying to get a reaction, because the lions – Faith, Hope and Charity

– were all lying down. If he wanted to see lions in action, he certainly did; by the time Dad arrived on the scene, the coat was in shreds. It turned out that it wasn't the coat he was worried about so much as his train ticket, which was in the pocket!

Dad and one of the boys tried to get the three lionesses to go back in the den with the usual trick of giving them a bone, but they weren't persuaded and continued prowling around the cage. Then, while they were shaking the shreds of what had once been a coat, a ticket fell on the ground, and the man had to watch as one of them put out her tongue and devoured it.

In March 1943 I said goodbye to Nixon's. Now that the zoo was no longer under threat, I'd decided to give up hairdressing. I never learnt how to cut or do a perm. A shampoo and set was my limit. For the first time in my life, I became an official employee of Chester Zoo, earning 10/- a week.

My first job was to collect an animal from Liverpool docks. Nothing to do with Miss Holt this time, but Dad had received a call from HM Customs. A sailor was being transferred to another vessel, and had been refused permission to take his pet monkey with him, so it needed a home.

So yet another bus journey, this time going north to Birkenhead, and then the ferry across the Mersey. I had never done this journey before – with Dad, we had always driven in the Hillman – and, as we crossed the river, I could see funnels sticking out of the water, ships that must have been bombed while they were in harbour. Once on the Liverpool side, I took the overhead railway north to the docks, which faced the open sea. It ran on electricity, not steam like other trains, and was known as the Docker's Umbrella, as it was about sixteen feet off the ground.

There is always tight security at any dock you go to, but in wartime it was ten times worse. By the time I arrived at the barrier, I was shaking with fear. People were always being told to watch out for German saboteurs and a 16-year-old girl would have been a good 'cover'.

'I've come to collect a monkey,' I said.

'I'm afraid I'll need a bit more than that, Miss.'

'It's a vervet monkey, originally from East Africa but introduced into the Caribbean. It has a grey body, black face, what look like white eyebrows and is vegetarian.'

'Very interesting, but not what I meant. I need the name of the ship and the name of the party.'

Only then did I remember to hand over the letter Dad had given me.

Apparently the Port of Liverpool was then

seven miles long. I didn't walk that far, though it was a long way and felt even longer because of the wolf-whistles and 'comments' as I passed. Before setting off, I hadn't given a thought about what to put on, but as it was a warm day, I was wearing a cotton frock and a cardigan. If these had been sailors who hadn't seen anyone of the opposite sex for months, I might have understood, but they were dockers, with wives and girlfriends down the road. I kept looking straight ahead and pretended I was deaf. Eventually I reached the gangplank, where a customs officer was waiting, and after a few minutes a sailor came down it, carrying a cardboard box tied with string.

Then I had to walk back.

Luckily the same policeman was on duty at the barrier, so I was let through without too much delay. He just looked through one of the air holes and said, 'I'll take your word for it.'

I hadn't been in Liverpool since the Blitz. I'd seen newsreels at the cinema, but looking at it in real life made you wonder how it could ever be rebuilt. There were parts that were just like shells after a fox had been at the eggs. Nothing in them and half of it missing. You couldn't imagine a building with rooms and stairs and life going on inside.

The journey back was even more stressful than before because this time I had the monkey and it had started to move, its weight shifting around all the time. It was only when I was safely on the bus at Birkenhead that I felt I could breathe freely. Luckily I got a window seat and jammed the box up in the rack alongside it. I felt exhausted but pleased that everything had gone according to plan. I'd soon be home.

About halfway there, we slowed down at a bus stop, and the woman beside me got up, leaning over to get her shopping from the rack above my head.

'Something must be broken in there,' she said.

I looked up to where she was pointing. It was the box.

'It's dripping. Look, on your woolly. You need to do something before it gets any worse.'

A quick sniff told me all I needed to know. There is no mistaking the tang of urine. The moment she left, I reached up to get the box down. When my hands touched the bottom I knew I couldn't put it on the empty seat beside me, so it stayed on my lap. But what if the bottom disintegrated? I decided I would rather walk than lose the monkey, so I got off a stop early. As my clothes were now reeking of monkey pee anyway, I took off my cardigan and tied it round the box by knotting the sleeves together. That would keep it secure at least. The moment I got

home and had changed, I dumped everything in the sink in the scullery and doused
it with half a bottle of disinfectant.

'I see you got the monkey,' Dad said when
he passed me in the passage.

'Yes, but...' He didn't stop to listen.

From the moment the two bison arrived
from Dudley Zoo early in 1940, they had
been nothing but trouble, especially Ferdinand the bull. His wife had given birth to a
calf a year after they'd arrived, but she had
died, so by the mid-40s there was just the
father and his four-year-old son, both as bad
as each other. Ferdinand and Billy were both
so strong that they could break through
anything if they felt like it. They could jump
over fences like steeplechasers and what they
couldn't jump, they pushed through. They
were always getting out, usually heading
straight for the lawn, which they lost no time
in churning up. Our first job in the morning
would be to get them back into their paddock
before visitors arrived. I found that if you
charged at them, running like mad, they
would retreat to the safety of their pen of
their own accord. Mum, Kay and I could get
them back in, but not Dad. There was something about my father that Ferdinand took
exception to, and the moment he caught
sight of him, Ferdinand would give chase and
Dad had to run for safety.

I am sure they knew what they were doing. They would stay happily in their enclosure all day and only once the zoo was empty again would they venture out. As with so many animals, they saw the fence as being for their benefit – to keep visitors at a safe distance.

As a first step, Dad attempted to divide their field in two using some second-hand fencing he had been given. While he and Kay were driving in the posts, Ferdinand took no notice, but no sooner had they walked away than Ferdinand would go over and investigate. If a post was not secured, he would toss it up in the air or roll it away as far as possible. Then, when they came back, he would stand and watch them search for the things he had moved. Dad was convinced he enjoyed making life difficult.

The obvious solution in the short term would have been to reinforce the existing fence, but any kind of metal or wire was unattainable. In 1942 Dad had written to the Ministry of Agriculture for permission to buy barbed wire for pens. They wrote back advising him to write to the Board of Trade, who in turn advised him to write to the War Office, who then sent him back to the Ministry of Agriculture...

Another pressing accommodation problem was that of the bears. Trotsky the Russian bear and Won Lung the Himalayan bear had been babies when they'd arrived in 1938 and 1939 respectively. Dad had hoped they could be quartered together, for companionship, but Won Lung had been so frightened of Trotsky – even though he was very under-sized – that it couldn't be done. Now, four years later, they were both adults in the peak of condition, even though their diet was largely limited to bread, lettuce and milk from the goats, and because of the problems of space, it was decided to try again to put them together, but the enclosure would have to be big enough.

Finally, in 1944, my father applied for permission to build a new bear pit. Not only were they a danger to the public in their present cage, which was falling to bits, the new one would require less in the way of building materials, especially steel, than re-pairing the old one. He was given the go-ahead and was allocated some concrete. Because of the lack of staff, it took time and Won Lung continued to escape, though usually it was enough to show her the pitch-fork and she'd retreat back to her pen without further ado.

One evening we heard Won Lung was out again, so Kay and I went to put her back in. It was a job that always needed two, one to brandish the pitchfork and chivvy her back in the right direction, the other to open the door. On this occasion it was Kay who showed her the pitchfork and, as it had no effect and she appeared set on continuing on her way out of the zoo, he gave a little prod. She turned round and grudgingly headed back the way she'd come, but she was not in a good mood. Just then Mum turned up with some bread and honey. Not realising there'd been a contretemps, and assuming Won Lung was her usual placid self, she went right up to her, holding out the snack, at which Won Lung struck out, knocked Mum to the ground and fell on top of her. Kay reacted by instinct, prodding the bear with his pitchfork to get her off.

I think Won Lung was so shocked by what she'd done that she went straight back to the enclosure. Mum got up and brushed herself down, more embarrassed than anything else, and said it was her fault and not Won Lung's. As we walked back to the house, I realised she was limping quite badly. Having done several first aid courses by this time, I knew what to do and ran her a bath, into which I poured an entire packet of salt. I also poured her a medicinal whisky.

'You know I don't drink, June,' she said, 'and I don't intend to start now.'

So I drank it myself, as by this point I was shaking more than she was. When you live in a zoo you can be lulled into a false sense of security – that these animals are your friends, that they will do you no harm. My mother had devoted her life to their well-being. And now this. It had shaken me to the core. There's no doubt in my mind that had it not been for Kay acting so quickly, my mother could have been killed. He had saved her life.

Although she had always been an intensely private person, I persuaded her to show me where she'd been hurt. The wound consisted of two deep puncture marks from the bear's incisors and four smaller bite marks on her thigh. She said it was nothing, but for once I took no notice and rang Dr Doby. He couldn't do much, he said. We just had to keep the wound clean and dry. After he left, Mum got dressed and went straight back to work.

Dad's original answer to the problem of keepers was to employ women, but now the country's first priority was war work and it didn't matter what sex you were as long as you could do the job. Although you could join up at seventeen and a half, once you were eighteen it was compulsory. So the girls who came straight from school as keepers, or to work in the office or in the café, never stayed long. They would get a letter from the Ministry of Labour and would have to leave to do 'work of national importance'.

By the spring of 1944 Dad had decided it was time for Mowgli to do work of importance for the zoo. He'd resisted it before because Mowgli's friendship with Peter was such a crowd-pleaser and the source of positive press coverage, which he saw as equally important. They were still a huge visitor attraction – especially when Peter tried to copy Mowgli in attempting to roar. But several months earlier Mowgli and Peter had been moved to a closed-in cage, rather than their pen. Just as Peter had rejected life as a normal dog, Mowgli had become aggressive whenever he was within sight or hearing of other lions.

Whenever Mowgli heard the other lions roar, he would answer them, then race up and down the fence, and there was a fear that he might actually jump over it. At the back of his enclosure was the original loose box where he and Peter would shelter if the weather was bad, and it was decided to put them in there while a travelling crate was organised. Mowgli knew something was going on, and before anyone knew what had happened, he had jumped nine feet onto a beam. It was only thanks to Peter that he was persuaded to come down.

The zoo's lion-breeding programme had stopped at the beginning of the war, but when it was clear that the raids had ended, Dad had brought in an adult male – Nero – an exchange from Bristol Zoo. Since his arrival in October 1941 Nero had sired eight cubs – six of whom had survived – but their character, like their father's, left a lot to be desired. Nero had caused more fights than any other lion the zoo had ever had, so when cubs were born, the keepers removed him from the cage. They knew Nero's temper. One cuff and they'd be dead. He had already killed two he'd sired by Faith's daughter Coral – and it wasn't worth taking the risk of losing anymore. When Faith herself had two cubs by Nero, it was the nice-tempered Patrick, her former husband, who stayed with her in the den during those first weeks when the cubs were most vulnerable and needed protection.

And then Nero died, and on 10 August 1943 – the evening of Granny and Granddad's golden wedding anniversary – Dad told me he'd come to a difficult decision. Peter and Mowgli were going to be parted. He needed more cubs and the only other male now available was Patrick, who couldn't be mated with his own daughters. Mowgli, as everyone knew, was a gentle creature and, like Patrick, would turn out to be a good father and produce handsome and amiable cubs, which would go some way to meeting the demand. And as the sale price then was £50 each, it would add considerably to the zoo's income.

Although I wasn't unhappy about this, I didn't feel easy either. Only a few months before, Mowgli had trodden on Peter's paw and torn his skin. People had always said that once Mowgli had tasted blood, that would be it – but it wasn't. He spent the next few days licking the wound clean and their relationship remained just as cordial, if not more so.

For the next few weeks, Peter was put in with several Dalmatians the zoo had been given. He couldn't be allowed to roam freely, Dad said, because he might think that all lions were friendly and find his way into the den at the back of the lion house... It had all turned out exactly as I had feared.

Mowgli was introduced to the lionesses and sired three cubs, though he didn't live to see them. He became so overwrought and agitated, he'd got himself into a sweat and caught a chill, which rapidly turned into pneumonia. A paraffin stove was brought into his cage, but the weather turned so cold it barely had an effect and the wind kept blowing it out. His condition worsened and after three days it was decided to let Peter in. So Peter was lying beside his friend as Mowgli slipped into unconsciousness. He died the next morning. As for Peter, he was put back with the Dalmatians. I would take him out for walks, but he was never allowed to roam freely again. Eventually, shortly after the war ended, he tunnelled his way out of the pen and came up in the next compound, where there were dingoes. He was killed instantly. I said then that I would never have another dog. And I didn't.

Chapter 11

Punch was now the oldest animal in the zoo. When he was sold to Dr English in 1930 he had been about twenty-five years old, so he was now coming up to forty – a very old bear. At least he was no longer on his own. In 1939 – shortly after he'd been adopted by Miss Tomkyns Grafton – he'd been joined by Judy, a much younger female who'd arrived as an evacuee when Butlin's holiday camp at Skegness was requisitioned by the Ministry of War. When they were first introduced, he was wary, but Judy didn't seem that concerned and immediately made for the small pool and splashed around, emerging refreshed and clean. Punch looked on, but made no attempt to follow suit. Every time she went in, he would watch with interest, but could not be persuaded to try this novelty himself.

Since appointing herself Punch's guardian in 1939, Miss Tomkyns Grafton had visited him several times a year to follow his progress and had been delighted when Judy had shown up and had willingly taken on the cost of feeding them both, which came to £1 week.

Over the years she had became increasingly concerned that while Judy was clean, Punch seemed determined to stay his familiar slush colour. She became convinced it was related to the size of the pool. It was just too small, she said, for him to have a proper wash and she would be happy to foot the bill if Mr Mottershead would consider building a bigger one.

The construction of the bear pit for Trotsky and Won Lung was the perfect opportunity, Dad realised. They would be done as a pair – both being built on the ditch-and-moat principle, with unclimbable walls. He would run a drive through the field that now housed the bison and both bear pits would be at the end of it. They would be comparatively cheap, as they would be made entirely out of stone and cement, with no upkeep costs. In addition, it would have the usual advantage of giving an unobstructed view to spectators. But it was a mammoth task and a system to circulate and filtrate the water was needed.

On the evening of 6 June, I was in the courtyard, helping Kay sort out the new howdah for Molly's rides – she had now grown sufficiently to take several children each side – when Mum ran in, out of breath.

'They've done it!'

'Done what, Mum?'

'They've crossed the Channel!'

It was Operation Neptune, the Normandy landings or D-Day, as it would forever after be known – the beginning of the end.

We had sensed something was imminent because, for the last week or so, the bypass had been nose-to-tail with convoys full of American troops. There had been no weather forecasts on the radio for some time – nothing that might give the Germans prior notice of good weather, essential for an invasion. Listeners had been asked to send in any holiday snaps or postcards they had of the entire French coastline. But nobody knew where or when it was likely to happen.

The commander in overall charge was General Eisenhower and the BBC repeated his announcement at regular intervals for the rest of the day.

People of Western Europe. A landing was made this morning on the coast of France by the troops of the allied expeditionary force... This landing is just the first of many battles that lie ahead. I call on all who love freedom to stand with us now, keep your faith staunch. Our armies are resolute. Together we shall achieve victory.

Later that week we all poured into the Majestic to watch the newsreel. It was packed, and when we emerged – tearful from both pride and sorrow – there were queues round the block for the next showing. Shortly after midnight on 5 June, 45,000 troops had been parachuted into Normandy. Naval bombardment of the coast started when it was still dark. Then, at daybreak, 7,000 boats and landing craft had begun to open up bridgeheads, protected by 9,500 aircraft.

Everyone, including it turned out the Germans, had thought the invasion would be across from Folkestone or Dover, the narrowest part of the English Channel. But Calais and Boulogne, the two ports on the French side, were heavily fortified. It was hard to land anywhere on the French coast, as it was so well defended. There were no big ports on that bit of Normandy – the main reason why the Germans didn't really expect them to land there – and we marvelled at the temporary Mulberry harbours, as they were called, invented by British engineers and towed across the Channel to enable tanks and supplies to be rolled off. One, known as Port Winston, near Arromanches, remained the only route into Europe for the next ten months, until Antwerp was taken. One and a half million men and half a million vehicles would enter France across floating roadways supported by concrete caissons and inflatable jetties that had been towed across from England.

It was terrible to think of all the casualties. A thousand Germans were killed that first day, but allied casualties were ten times that.

It was distressing to realise that so many had lost their lives with the end so nearly in sight. We all thought that the allies would advance quicker than they did. We thought it would be a question of weeks before Hitler capitulated. But General Montgomery, who was in charge on the ground, predicted that it would take ninety days to reach the River Seine, and he was right. Paris was liberated on 25 August 1944.

By D-Day I had already received my call-up papers. Like Muriel, I had decided to join the Wrens, but sadly I failed the medical – some kind of heart murmur, I was told – and I was sent to work at the munitions factory in Liverpool Road.

Before the war Williams & Williams had made steel window frames, now it made jerry cans – metal containers for transporting petrol. With no fuel available in France, this would be as important as anything when it came to the push to Berlin. In fact the design had been stolen from the Germans; it allowed petrol to be poured into a tank without the need for funnels, and the positioning of the handles meant it could be carried by either one or two people, or even passed down a human chain.

Along with everyone else, I was stationed at a conveyor belt, and it was noisy, dusty and monotonous work. Three times a week, at lunchtime, there would be *Workers' Playtime* on the radio, broadcast live from a works' canteen 'somewhere in Britain'. When that wasn't on, we had *Music While You Work*. Sometimes variety artists would come and entertain us. For all this, I hated it and applied to join the Women's Land Army.

Perhaps because I had some experience of horticulture, I was sent to a nursery in Delamere, about ten miles east of Chester. The area is very beautiful: an ancient forest with dozens of meres – small lakes – dotted around it. Nearby a large estate called Delamere Park had been turned into an American army base housing over 10,000 troops, and you'd see them on the roads, setting out in convoy for France. It never let up – wave after wave would go out.

I had been sent to a country house called Sandymere, not so different to Oakfield, with a croquet lawn, a lake and a heather garden. There were a couple of other girls and, as we were billeted there, the owners had to feed us. Our uniform consisted of brown corduroy breeches, an aertex shirt and green jumper, long fawn socks, sturdy shoes, a greatcoat, an oilskin mac and a felt hat.

We slept in the attic. The chair beside my bed had a loose leg, but I was often so tired I would forget and sit on it and invariably end up sprawling on the floor, with barely the energy to get up. The day started at six. Before setting off, we'd go down to the kitchen to make up a sandwich of bread and cheese. The standard cheese ration was 2 oz a week, but as land girls, ours was upped to 12 oz a week. As far as I know, this was the only concession to our physical workload.

At the nursery I worked under the head gardener in the greenhouse. He set very high standards. He wouldn't tolerate any weeds – if he saw even a seedling he'd be down on you like a ton of bricks – and all the tools had to be washed and oiled and put in their correct places at the end of the day.

One of my jobs was fertilising the tomato plants, making sure the stamens of the little white flowers were dusted with pollen, using a rabbit's tail on the end of a stick. I'd often watched Granddad do this, and so I picked it up quickly. It was the same with removing the side shoots. At the start they'd be sprawling all over the place, but once tied up with string to a wooden frame, they looked like soldiers standing to attention. It was all very satisfying, and I loved the smell – it took me back to those days when I'd escape to the kitchen garden with Jet and have long conversations about auriculas with Granddad.

The other girls had been in the land army for longer than I had and came from all kinds of backgrounds, but we all mucked in, and it wasn't long before I could honestly say I was happy. The worst job was forking manure around the fruit trees in the orchard

– acres and acres of them – and I developed blisters on my hands. I didn't mind the physical work – of course I was more used to it than some of the others. Even the ones who looked stuck up weren't really. We were all in it together, and it was a revelation. They even took me to the local pub! I had once stayed the night with Zena above her father's pub on the Duke of Westminster's estate, but we never actually went in it. 'Nice' girls didn't do that kind of thing in those days. It took the war to change all that. It felt like real freedom. However, for me, it would be short-lived. It turned out that I'd only been sent as a replacement for someone else, so I had to leave after only six weeks.

My next posting was at Hoole Hall, barely a mile from the zoo, so I would spend the nights at home and bike there every morning. At Sandymere I'd enjoyed the camaraderie and companionship of the other girls. Now I had all the work but none of the fun, because once I got back to Oakfield, I'd have to help in the café, clearing up and getting ready for the next day.

Hoole Hall was an eighteenth-century mansion surrounded by gardens and farmland, and I worked there for just over a year. I was put to work doing similar jobs in the greenhouses as I'd done at Delamere. I looked after the tomatoes and we also grew lettuces and, as July turned to August, there were blackcurrants to pick, when my fingers turned blue. Then began the work in the fields, which was back-breaking in comparison – picking potatoes, field after field. And so the winter went on. Each day was like the last and the next. Rain or shine, it made no difference, we still had to be out there, though the mud made lifting root vegetables twenty times more difficult.

On 6 May 1945 we were thinning turnips when one of the lads came racing across the field towards us, waving his hands in the air.

'It's over!' he shouted. 'It's over! The Germans have surrendered!' For about five minutes, we all hugged each other. There were tears and laughter, then more tears. But there was no downing tools until the usual time to pack up. During the war years the country had double summer time, so that the light would last until ten in order to bring in the harvest. But after the day's work was over, I pedalled like a demon back to the zoo, rushed upstairs, got changed and cycled back into Chester, as I'd planned to meet Rachel, another land girl who worked at Hoole. I'd also phoned Nancy and arranged to rendezvous with her and Margaret, who were both working on their mother's farm. Above all, this was a day when you wanted to be with your friends.

The streets of Chester were jammed with people milling around, chatting, singing, hugging – being kissed by complete strangers, especially service men. Everyone was jubilant – happy and relieved that Germany had been defeated. We all knew that this didn't mean it was over. We were still at war with the Japanese and many people had menfolk who were still out there fighting or in prisoner-of-war camps. But for one night we allowed ourselves to forget everything except V for Victory. The celebrations that night were completely spontaneous and went on until the small hours. But the next day it was back to work as normal.

When I'd rushed home to get out of my uniform, I don't think I even spoke to my parents, because it was a big day at Chester Zoo – the official opening of both the polar-bear pool and the bear enclosure. The bears had actually been ensconced in their new quarters for several days – it had taken 30,000 gallons of water, drawn from an artesian well that Dad had sunk, to fill the polar bears' pool. But Punch had still not taken the plunge. The night before, Dad had been going mad. How could we inveigle Punch to go in? It was Miss Tomkyns Grafton he was thinking about, as she was to be the guest of honour. And she'd done all this just for Punch, just to see him swimming.

Around lunchtime Dad drove into Chester to pick her up from the station. Mum offered her a cup of tea and a scone when they arrived, but she was anxious to see Punch, she said. The ground around the new enclosures was still quite churned up after the building works, and as they picked their way through the dried mud, Dad's heart sank.

Both polar bears were sitting on top of their rock, as if ready to give a performance. Miss Tomkyns Grafton surveyed the scene and said, in her rather prim voice, 'Now come along, you two! Let me see how you like your new home.'

As if by royal command, the bears shambled to the side of the pool and slid in, waves splashing all around, and were soon besporting themselves as if they were kids at the seaside, Dad said. Miss Tomkyns Grafton stayed a few minutes, watching them, nodded quietly to herself, then turned away and said she'd take up Mum's offer of a cup of tea, but then she'd have to be going. She had a long journey up to the Lake District ahead of her and she wasn't getting any younger, she explained.

On the way back to Chester Station she was quiet, Dad said. Only when he had put her on the train and they were saying good-bye did she speak.

'Well, I think this is probably it, Mr Mottershead, as I won't be seeing you again. But I want to thank you for all you have done for Punch. Now that he has had a bath, I can die in peace.'

She passed away quietly in her sleep six months later, on 27 November 1945, aged eighty-three, leaving 'a substantial sum' to the North of England Zoological Society in her will. As dad was quoted in the local paper, 'It will be sufficient to put the zoo on its feet.' This was a rare understatement from my father. It was a little over £18,000, the bulk of her estate, once smaller bequests had been carried out, five times what Oakfield had cost in 1930. Miss Tomkyns Grafton had lived alone on the shores of Lake Windermere, in a village called Far Sawrey, famous as the home of Beatrix Potter, who was born the same year and had died two years earlier. I used to wonder if they knew each other, and I like to think they did.

A few weeks later it was the hay harvest at Hoole. The weather was an English summer at its most glorious and at least now I wasn't wearing heavy corduroys, but dungarees cut off at the knee. First the hay was cut by a horse-drawn mower until it lay in great swathes over the ground. Then we moved along the rows, turning the loose hay so it would dry in the sun, then raked it into small piles called ricks. Finally, using pitchforks, we threw it into the back of a horse-drawn wagon, where one of the girls would be standing to load it up.

The wheat harvest came much later, left until it was golden and the heads were drooping with the weight of the grain. After being cut it was stored in the loft above one of the barns until the threshing machine arrived. Then we'd climb up the ladder and pitchfork it down into the waiting jaws, where it would be shaken to loosen the grain from the hard outer husk.

I could remember watching my uncles do it by hand in the thirties. They only grew a small amount of wheat on Bower's Farm – just sufficient to see the poultry through the winter – and I can still see my uncles flailing it on the floor, using long-handled sticks with a string attached and a small piece of wood at the end. I would keep my distance, as I didn't want to be hit. It would take hours to thresh just a small quantity and it was hard work, even for strong men like them. Now it was being done in a tenth of the time.

The final stage was the winnowing, when the chaff was blown off. It was like being in a dust storm, the air so thick you could barely see. I stuck it out for as long as I could, but when I could no longer breathe I was sent home. It must have been some kind of allergy, I think. But it was enough to give me a discharge and I went back to the zoo. At first I was ill, but the moment Dad considered I was better, he said it was about time the aquarium was sorted out, so I set to work. It never occurred to me to do anything else.

Closed since the autumn of 1940, it was staggering just how much junk had accumulated down there. The cellars were also liable to flood in a heavy downpour and although there was a hand pump, nobody had had the time to do it and the water had been allowed to subside naturally, which meant it was very damp. It took some months, but eventually I got to the stage of filling the tanks with water again. Most of them leaked. I tried to stop the leaks with clay, which was partially successful; the ones I failed to make watertight, I turned into vivariums for our collection of amphibians. A member called Mr Parker – an electrician by trade – would come and stay every weekend and, just for his keep, did all the electrical work. He cannibalised an old fridge compressor to make an aeration system.

Granddad's conservatory, which had doubled as the reptile house, had suffered irreparable damage and sadly had to be demolished, so it was decided to build a new entrance and exit with its own pay box and use all the cellars and incorporate the snake pens down there. This new exhibit would bring in an additional six pence entrance fee, which would enhance the revenue. However, that lay in the future. The number of tropical fish available at the time was limited, so I set about breeding what few I could with the help of a handbook called *Life and Love in an Aquarium* by C. H. Peters, which Peter Falwasser had given me. Fish may breed more quickly than mammals, but to build up a collection from scratch takes time.

Cassandra had been the first lion born at Chester zoo, daughter of Faith and Patrick. She was also one of the naughty cubs who'd killed the sheep. But in maturity she had proved a very good mother, bearing six healthy litters. Her cubs had been sold for a total of £470.

This would be Cassandra's seventh litter – all the other births had gone smoothly and there was no reason to suspect the latest would be any different. On the contrary, at six years old, she was a veteran and knew what she was doing. She went into labour on Christmas Eve morning, but the first cub – a male – was stillborn. Then, a few minutes later, a second one emerged – a female and alive. There were clearly other cubs still inside, waiting to be born – her last litter had yielded six babies – but after many hours it was decided she needed help. By the following day there was still no sign of the others and she was so exhausted that she died, and the remaining cubs died with her.

That evening we sat around the fire, wondering what to do. Dad was cradling the little cub on his lap, wrapped in an old piece of blanket, with a nose peeking out. The little body was barely moving. The chances of it surviving, he said, were negligible.

'We'll never rear it,' he sighed. 'Not without Muriel.'

'What about me?' I said.

'You wouldn't know what to do.'

'I don't know why you say that, Dad. I helped before.'

'But that was nearly six years ago.'

There had been other cubs at the zoo – twenty in total – since the war, but they had all been reared by their resident mothers and neither I nor anyone else had touched them until they were considerably older. If a lioness smelled the hand of a human there was a very good chance that the cub would be rejected. We would only step in if the cubs were at risk. The last orphan at the zoo had been Victor/Mowgli.

But I did remember what to do. I had given orphan lion cubs their bottles when Muriel was busy. It was true that you didn't get much sleep, but that seemed a small price to pay for saving a life.

'Please, Dad, let me try.'

He looked down at the helpless little creature in his lap. Its eyes weren't even open. As the only other option was to have her put down, he reluctantly agreed.

I named her Christy.

Christy was the most beautiful lion cub in the world. Her fur was golden, and thick and soft. She had huge paws and a loud purr. I did everything I remembered from watching Muriel. For the first week or so I gave her a bottle every few hours, warm milk, just like a human baby. I found her a box and filled it with straw and kept her well wrapped up in a wool blanket. During the day I would pop up from the cellar every half an hour or so to check on her. At night she would sleep in an old rectangular aviary beside my bed. By the time she was three months old, she was fully house-trained, using a tray of wood ash from the fire in the sitting room that helped keep her warm, and she knew her name when I called her. Once she started to walk, I carried on as usual, but she would follow me down to the cellar when I was busy in the aquarium.

To wean her, I fed her morsels of horse-meat, then bigger chunks, until eventually she would take a bone with flesh on it. Although she never put her claws out when playing with us, she made up for it on the mahogany dining chairs. She would sit on them back to front, hang her paws over the top and then chew the rail.

As she continued to grow, she would jump on your back and at first it was fun, but then she became too heavy and I'd buckle at the knees.

There were other things to do besides the aquarium. Granddad was now very old – and the garden was in a sorry state, having not been top of the list of priorities for many years, and had quite gone to seed. My job was now just to clear it up, including the pond by the lodge, which was clogged up and stinky – the birds had all disappeared during the first air raid in August 1940. Although Granddad was always there to give me advice, I was now Oakfield's de facto gardener.

Granddad was now living on his own at the lodge, as Granny had died in April 1945, aged eighty-five. The last years of her life had been very sad, as her memory had quite gone. But Granddad never stopped loving her. You would see them sitting together on the bench outside the lodge in the afternoon sun, chatting to visitors as they walked by. But at least she had seen her son realise his dream of building a zoo. It was only a pity that the war years had taken their toll and the zoo was only a shabby relic of its 1939 self.

Christy was now too big for me to carry – but it made no difference, she would follow wherever I went, like the lamb in the nursery rhyme. If I needed to leave the grounds, Mum would take her inside and keep her calm until I was out of sight, but I'd hear the yowling from halfway up the drive.

I knew exactly what she'd do while I was away: she'd pad up and down, wandering around the house, looking for me, going in and out of every room and ending up sleeping on my bed. But when she was six months old, even though she was fully house-trained, Dad decided she was too big to be in the house and he'd had enough, he said, of chewed furniture.

'You of all people should understand,' he said one evening. 'She needs to learn that she's a lion. I don't want the same thing to happen to her as happened to Mowgli.'

But when Dad put her in the lion enclosure with the others for the first time, she hissed and howled. So then they put her in a cage on her own. And she still howled. Visitors would ask if she was ill. She wasn't. She just wanted to be in the house or with me.

The moment the last visitor had gone, I'd go straight to Christy's cage and let her out. She was now so strong that when she jumped up to put her paws on my shoulders, she'd knock me over. But never once did she put out her claws or try to bite me.

But Dad wasn't happy. He gave instructions that she was not to be allowed out unless he was there.

'You must understand, June. Christy is not

a kitten. She's a lion. She might be quite safe with you, but what would happen if she took it into her head to go exploring in the village?'

'She wouldn't. She'd stay with me.'

'I'm sorry, but I can't risk it. If the villagers had any idea there was a fully grown lion roaming the grounds, we would be finished.'

'But she's not fully grown.'

'They wouldn't know that.'

My mum was really torn. She knew how I loved Christy and that she would never do me any harm.

And Christy was so happy when she heard me coming. When she heard the keys rattling in my hand she would yawn and prance, waiting for that moment when the door was opened and she could bound out. I used to love those evenings, with long shadows striping the lawns, with Mum doing her rounds with titbits for the animals walking behind us, not even trying to keep up. I remember laughing and running across the grass, playing hide and seek in the bushes, when Christy would creep up on me and then pounce, or hook a paw around my leg and pull me over.

Every time Dad went out it was like our secret, and Kay didn't let on. Like anyone who truly loves animals as he did, he wanted to see Christy happy and we'd always have her back in her cage by the time Dad returned. Of course, when it came to that moment, she would be extremely reluctant to go in. She would lie down flat and refuse to move, so we had to make her. Mum would take the front legs and I would take the back and we'd carefully drag her into the pen.

This sneaking her out went on for months – in fact for almost a year. Nobody knew except Mum, Kay and me, because the young keepers would have gone home before we let her out.

One evening I went with Dad to collect a crested crane that had landed in someone's garden several miles away. They'd phoned to ask someone to come and collect it, and it was easier with the two of us.

Doing her usual nightly round, Mum had passed Christy's cage and decided to let her out. Christy was so beautiful, just to see her bounding across the grass, being playful with the other animals, was a tonic, Mum used to say. Not one of them was frightened of her. Mum would usually take out a supply of stale bread, to give as titbits, but that evening, when she got to Bambi, the little fallow deer, she realised she'd run out, so went back to the house to get some more, leaving Christy and Bambi playing together.

By the time she returned, although Bambi was still there, Christy was gone.

I only heard about what happened later.

Mum had called and called Christy's name, but nothing. She became more and more agitated as she searched the grounds, looking in all the places Christy might hide, thinking it was a game: in the laurels, by the pond near the lodge... Nothing. She found Kay sitting in the kitchen with Dorothy, said that she had something to discuss with him and then the two of them scoured the grounds, calling Christy's name.

'We'll have to try the farms, Mrs Mott... Perhaps we should call someone,' Kay said.

'Not yet,' said my mother. 'Not yet.' She knew what it would mean if word got out that a lion was on the loose. Distraught, she went back to the house, leaving Kay searching the adjacent fields, looking for flattened barley or anything that would give a clue as to where she had gone.

Just as Mum got back to the house, terrified of what Dad would say, terrified of what might happen if Christy should come across an animal or a child, Marjorie emerged from the garden door. She'd just come back from seeing a friend.

'Mrs Mott?'

'Not now, Marjorie. I can't talk now,' Mum said, steeling herself for the phone call she knew she'd have to make to the police.

'But, Mrs Mott, what's Christy doing in the house? You know Mr Mott said it had

300

to stop.'

Mum stepped in her tracks. 'What did you say?'

'That Mr Mott said it should stop.'

'Before that...'

'Christy. She's upstairs in Nathalie's room, asleep.'

And then Mum started crying and shaking. Kay and Dorothy's little girl was about eighteen months old – and this was where Christy had gone. She must have followed Mum in when she returned to the kitchen, looking for more bread, and Mum just hadn't seen her. All Christy had wanted was company.

Marjorie had carried the sleeping toddler down to her mother in the kitchen. She hadn't told her the truth. She didn't think it was a good idea... She'd left Christy where she was, but had closed the door. Mum then went to find Kay and together they took the sleepy lion back to her pen.

Kay knew Christy as well as anyone, but when it came to his own child... He couldn't go on with it anymore, he said. He'd seen how she could turn on someone because she'd turned on him when he'd gone into her cage one time. Fortunately, he'd had the presence of mind to take off his coat and fling it at her face.

'I think she could smell elephant on me,' he'd said.

When Dad and I got back, it was truly

terrible. It had been a wasted journey, as the crane had flown off by the time we arrived and was already back on our lawn. We were met by Mum in tears. Until then, Dad had had no idea that we had been taking Christy out all this time without his knowledge. I had never seen him so angry.

'Is that what you want for Christy?' he said to me. 'To have her shot? Because, mark my words, my girl, that's what will happen.'

There would be no more special treatment, he decided. She would have to go in the main enclosure with the others. She was old enough to become a mother, he said. 'And once she's got cubs of her own, things will change, you'll see.'

They decided to wait until most of the visitors had gone for the day. Dad told me to go down to the aquarium and keep out of it. Down there, I could hear nothing, just the faint hiss of the aeration system. I only heard what happened later from Kay. The moment they forced her into the enclosure with the other lionesses and the gate had shut behind her, she'd gone for the first one who'd approached her. Suddenly they were all snarling and fighting. Christy escaped by climbing a tree, but the others continued to prowl round the trunk. Afraid it would be a bloodbath and he'd lose them all, Dad got Kay to tempt them back into the den with bones. They couldn't have been less interested and stayed growling and baring their teeth at the foot of the tree. There was only one thing for it, Dad decided. He would have to go in there himself. He knew about the incident with Kay and Christy, but she had never shown any aggression towards him. At the sound of the bolt and the hinge, the lionesses turned their attention to the interloper. Armed only with a pitchfork, he walked slowly towards them, sweeping them backwards towards their den. Once they were safely enclosed, Christy came down and allowed Dad to put her back in her cage.

I heard raised voices upstairs in the kitchen and couldn't stop myself running up. Dad looked at me, shook his head, then left the room, and I heard him go upstairs to the office.

'What happened?' I asked Mum.

'You'll have to ask Kay. I wasn't there.'

Kay was still at the lion house. Christy I saw, was in her own cage, which I hadn't been expecting. But something was different. She didn't come bounding over to me, but just sat in the corner and stared. I clung onto the mesh and wept and wept, until Kay fetched my Mum, who prised me away.

From then on, I wasn't allowed anywhere near her. No going to the lion house for any reason. I had work in the aquarium to do, Dad said, and then there was the garden.

Plenty to keep me occupied. Only then, when she'd got used to my not being there, could Christy have a chance of readjusting.

I don't know if she ever readjusted. I would just lie on my bed and cry, listening to her yowling and yowling. It was unbearable.

Dad never mentioned Christy by name to me again. I heard later that she'd been mated, but was now back living on her own. She gave birth to three cubs on 14 May 1948, probably fathered by Rory, a male who'd arrived from Dublin. The first died before it was realised she wasn't feeding it. The second two were taken from her and hand-reared. But not by me.

I would never get close to any animal again. Dad wouldn't let me – I wasn't mature enough to keep my distance, he said. And even if he'd asked me, I would have refused.

Christy left the zoo at the end of December 1950, in an exchange with a foreign zoo. Had I ruined her life? The question plagued me like a sore that wouldn't heal. Just like Mowgli thought he was a dog, Christy thought she was human, and it was my fault.

Even now, I grieve for her. I loved her so much and yet could do nothing to help her. I resolved that I would have nothing to do with any animal that was not mine again and I retreated to the aquarium. Although you can get attached to certain fish, there is never the same bond as with a warm-blooded animal.

How many loves do any of us have in one life? I loved Christy and it broke my heart.

Chapter 12

Rulers and conquerors have kept wild animals in captivity since before records began. Alexander the Great had stables of African and Indian elephants and was often presented with exotic animals as tribute from those whose lands he occupied, though the Greeks in general favoured cages of wild birds. Romans also took animals as spoils of war – the Emperor Trajan is reported to have had a collection of 11,000. At the end of the eighth century Emperor Charlemagne's menagerie was famed throughout the known world. Nor was it just a European thing. Menageries existed in ancient Egypt. Montezuma, the Aztec ruler conquered by the Spanish, had a huge collection. Falcons and cheetahs were kept for hunting in India.

From the time of Henry III, the Tower of London held the English royal collection – including lions and tigers – and when ambassadors needed a gift to present to the monarch, an exotic animal was always acceptable.

One of the most impressive collections was in Versailles. It had been incorporated into the architects' plans from the outset. This 'zoological garden', complete with shrubs and trees to disguise the bars, was soon as famous as the palace itself. Like everything that Louis XIV did, it was immediately copied, and soon no self-respecting aristocrat could do without one. Such collections were rarely seen by the public.

But then came the revolution, and Versailles represented everything evil about the old system. In October 1789 an angry – and probably hungry – mob arrived at the gates, demanding that the cages be opened and the animals killed for meat. But when faced with the reality of lions and tigers running amok, they changed their minds, although a few non-threatening animals were released in the spirit of the revolution.

Yet something had to be done with those that remained. What about the Jardin des Plantes? Originally it had been set up for the study of medicinal herbs, the university being next door. But with nowhere else remotely suitable, it became a de facto zoo, thirty-six animals arriving from the Duke of Orleans' estate alone. The Versailles collection eventually joined them, but not before money had been granted by the revolutionary government to build the necessary cages. One important proviso was attached to the money: the animals were to be available to ordinary citizens for the purposes of education and recreation. Thus the Jardin des Plantes in Paris became the first public zoo and the template for all that would follow, including ours.

Thanks to Miss Tomkyns Grafton's bequest, Chester Zoo had been able to buy more land on which it could eventually expand. However, until the food situation improved, it would be mainly used to grow crops. At the start of the war the zoo had had thirty-two acres. It now had an additional forty, including several natural ponds, which in 1948 would be turned into a waterfowl lake, complete with its own island.

After fifteen years of living in a state of perpetual crisis the zoo was now on a firm financial footing, so repairs and improvements could go ahead. The first project on my father's list was the lion enclosure. But after the most destructive war in Britain's history, towns and cities had to be rebuilt and people rehoused, so materials were in short supply.

Dad had been an advocate of make-do-and-mend long before it became government policy, and luckily he had one of his light-bulb moments. Near the coastline, as Chester was, anti-tank road blocks had been part of the country's defences against invasion. Not only were these no longer wanted, they were also in the way and would need to be shifted. He got through to someone at the

Ministry of Supply, who got through to someone else, and it was arranged. He would take as many as he wanted – road blocks and pill-boxes – for nothing. They were only too happy to get rid of them.

For that first stage we used over a thousand, and we continued to use them for years afterwards. The car park and every drive became a temporary resting place for the road blocks, and the pill-boxes were dumped on one of the newly bought fields. The road blocks were moved with the help of a shire horse called Spitfire, and then man-handled into place with the help of levers and block-and-tackle systems.

While the plan for the lion enclosure was not heavy on materials, Dad knew it would be labour intensive and he needed staff who would be as happy to work with cement as they would with animals. Luckily, now that the war was over, there were plenty of applicants.

There was Ziggy, who came in March 1947 and had escaped from Nazi-occupied Poland. He arrived via Hungary during the war and once the war was over he applied to stay in Britain. As this required him to have job, he came to work at the zoo.

Roberto Galarti was Italian, a former prisoner of war who had married an English girl – they eventually emigrated to Australia. Then there was a boy who was waiting for a passage back to Burma, whose name I've forgotten. Barbara Wright had worked at the zoo before she went into the land army. She was put in charge of the lions. Mrs Maddox was local – the first time anyone from Upton had worked at the zoo – and she did anything that was wanted, from men's work to waitressing in the café. And then there was Fred Williams and two other local boys. Fred was twenty-two and came as the bear keeper. I don't think one of them had any experience.

Someone who did was Charlie Collins, but he wasn't demobbed till a year later. The moment he came back, he was out working in the garden, but once he had it under control, he and Mrs Maddox built the reptile house and then he became the keeper, Granddad having taught him everything he knew.

Keepers or gardeners, whatever our jobs on paper, we would help with the building work – digging moats, moving road blocks, anything that was needed, learning as we went along. We didn't get paid overtime, nor did we ask for it, because we all knew we were helping to build the zoo.

Fred's first job was helping to move the anti-tank road blocks. Over just two days, he, Ziggy and Roberto – helped by Kay and Molly – hauled into place 118 of these lumps of concrete, each one weighing fourteen hundredweight – around 700 kilos. As well as marking the outer perimeter of the zoo, separating us from the riding school, they would also form the outer perimeter of the lion enclosure, each one being the base for a stanchion supporting the fencing that would be the only physical barrier between the lions and the public.

The area to be fenced was about an acre – the largest lion enclosure in Britain, exceeding even Whipsnade's – and, as always, materials were the problem. This was eventually solved when my father found some heavy-duty link netting, originally used for airfield runways. Even so, as the fence would need to be twelve-foot high, with a three-foot overhang, the quantity needed was considerable. Although RAF war surplus, it didn't come free, and was paid for by the generosity of one of the society's members, Miss Lois Bulley, who had recently given Ness Botanic Gardens, on the banks of the Dee Estuary, to the National Trust.

My father had three guiding principles when it came to keeping animals in captivity: light, fresh air and warmth. But facilities for visitors were also high on his agenda, and as well as being able to look through the fencing, a pillared shelter doubled as a viewing terrace, below which the lions would be fed.

The issue of light had long been a problem

with the old monkey house in the former stables, and this would be the next big project, allowing the zoo to rebuild its collection, which had been seriously depleted by the war. The new monkey house would also house the chimps and other great apes when we got them, and once that was achieved, the stables where all the animals had been kept in the early days would be closed to the public.

Fred Williams and I were thrown together when my dad sent him down to help me with the aquarium. He had the sunniest smile of anyone I had ever met. One evening we went looking for sticklebacks for the aquarium in the many ponds in the fields round about that were one positive result of the bombing raids in 1940. Although it may not sound the most obvious of romantic trysts, it did it for us.

I had had boyfriends before, but nothing you would call serious. The first boy I fell for was my cousin George. We had known each other since the early thirties, when he had lived at the lodge, and then, of course, he had marched with me in front of the elephants. So it had been quite strange when the feelings changed from cousinly to something else. Granny strongly disapproved, and so it never really went anywhere. During the war most young men were on the move – only farmers' sons stayed around. By the spring of

1947 I was going out with a demobbed soldier called John, who had just come back from Iraq, but once Fred arrived, we drifted apart.

The lion enclosure was officially opened on 28 May 1947. Among those watching the lionesses walk out into their wooded home for the first time were Gerard Iles of Belle Vue Zoo and Miss Geraldine Russell Allen, no longer in her matron's uniform. The ribbon was cut by 'Nomad', the BBC *Children's Hour's* resident naturalist, and his speech was recorded and broadcast on 16 June. It had taken only two months from start to finish. We had missed Easter, but were ready for Whitsun, and on Whit Monday over 2,000 people visited the zoo – the most we had ever had in one day.

Ten years had passed since the opposition to Dad's lion-enclosure scheme had put the whole future of a zoo without bars in jeopardy. But in spite of the Jeremiahs, the lions had never escaped, although five lionesses were once let out by mistake: a new keeper had opened the trap door in the inner den, not realising the outdoor enclosure wasn't yet finished. Fortunately the lionesses stayed in the shrubbery, and Dad and Kay put them back.

Fred and I were now 'courting', but in secret, although Mum had her suspicions. The more I got to know him, the more I liked him, and the luckier I felt that fate had brought us together. We spent hours talking about our lives – mine in the zoo and his extraordinary family. He'd had a very hard life. His father had died under anaesthetic when Fred was only six, after a routine extraction of wisdom teeth. He had seven older half-brothers from his father's first marriage. Their mother had died, leaving Fred's father with a young family. His father had worked for the GPO – and he was awarded the Croix de Guerre by the French government, for installing telegraph lines at the front during the First World War. He had met Fred's mother at Chester Station, where she had been the manager of the buffet, when he was coming back from France. They went on to have five children – two older than Fred, Bette and Frank, and two younger, Phyl and Jean. If that wasn't enough, his mother also looked after a baby called Beryl, whom she later adopted.

Fred was six months older than me. After leaving school he'd worked on the railways as a fireman. It was good money and a secure job, and he wanted to support his mum. He had always been a worker. At the age of twelve he took a job as a delivery boy with the local grocer's, even though he didn't know how to ride a bike and had to push it until he was big enough to reach the pedals.

Working for the railways was a reserved

occupation, so he wasn't called up, but he decided to volunteer for the RAF as soon as he turned eighteen. However, he never saw active service. He contracted pneumonia and was in hospital in Blackpool during the Normandy landings. When the war in Europe was over he returned to his former job, but once back, he hated it. He wanted to do more with his life, which was when he spotted Dad's ad for keepers in the local paper.

Fred had always loved animals and when little he would scour the family garden for beetles and caterpillars, not to destroy them, but just to examine them, always putting them gently back where he'd found them. He kept guinea pigs and birds, in an aviary he'd made himself, as well as fish and newts in a pond. He would sneak animals into the house whenever he could and would have filled the house if he'd been allowed to by his mother. As it was, he didn't do too badly, with an aviary with budgerigars and canaries on the landing. In the cellar he bred mice, which he sold to friends and neighbours, but he was careful only to sell same-sex pairs, so as to keep the monopoly on breeding. He was immensely practical and had learnt, from his older brothers at an early age, how to fix just about anything.

As for our courting, we did the usual things young people did in those days. We went dancing. Fred was never short of partners –

they called him Fairy Feet – and you could hardly have said that about me! We went ice-skating with his younger sister Jean and her boyfriend. We went to the pictures and sat in the back row of the stalls and would forget what film we were watching. One day we took the bus and walked up and down the promenade at New Brighton, holding hands, far enough away from the zoo not to bump into anyone we knew. During Chester race week we went to Collins Fair, on a site between the river and the old city walls, and wandered around the sideshows. There was a giraffe-necked woman and a spider woman, boxing booths and coconut shies, shove ha'penny boards and shooting galleries. We threw rings over goldfish bowls, but didn't win one. There was a ghost train, waltzers, even a big wheel.

Much of our spare time we spent away from prying eyes in the aquarium and often we'd be there long after everyone else had gone home – there were always odd jobs to be done. As the zoo was growing so rapidly, you felt a real sense of achievement when you knew you could improve things and make a difference. My twenty-first birthday was on 21 June 1947. Auntie Jessie had made a special trip from Didsbury and gave me a gold locket on a chain – a present from my cousin George, who was still in North Africa and had asked her to buy it for me. We never made a big fuss over birthdays in our family, so it was a day like any other, and my plan had been to have a small get-together later on, with just my family and the Lloyd sisters, but in the end only Nancy came, as Margaret had been invited on a date. Unfortunately a coach party of pensioners arrived at about seven in the evening, hoping to be fed. Mum would never turn anyone away, and as most of the café staff had gone home, Nancy and I were co-opted as waitresses. By the time we'd finished and had helped with the washing-up, we were too tired to celebrate. I felt very embarrassed that Nancy had had to help out, given I'd invited her over for a party.

The offer of new animals was always a mixed blessing, unless Dad knew well in advance that they were coming and could make the necessary arrangements. And in May 1947 had come news of two sea lions, Sammy and Susie, but unfortunately there was no accommodation. Fred was in charge of Won Lung and Trotsky, as well as Punch and Judy, so the burden of sorting it out went to him. As they had to have water, for several weeks, Sammy and Susie were housed in the polar bears' outdoor pen, while poor Punch and Judy were kept shut up inside their den.

Even with the help of a bulldozer, it took a month to get another enclosure built – a pool 200 feet long and 12 feet deep, dug out of the Cheshire clay and lined by thousands of concrete blocks and surrounded by chestnut paling. During the entire period Fred never took a day off. Keeping separate two polar bears and two sea lions, as well as Trotsky and Won Lung, took very careful management in the trapping procedure.

While giving the sea lions' temporary enclosure a clean, Fred had to climb in via a ladder and slipped. Having been designed for polar bears, the pool was about two metres deep, with a central rock set into concrete. In the two years since it had been built, algae had built up on the sides, making it danger-ously slippery. Time and time again he tried to get out, but his hands couldn't get a firm grip and he only succeeded in slipping fur-ther in, building up speed, until he slithered right to the bottom. Meanwhile Sammy and Susie were darting around him, intrigued at the floundering creature invading their pool.

Fortunately, Fred eventually found a spot neither too steep nor too slippery and man-aged to haul himself out. It might not have ended so well had he not been such a good swimmer, or if Sammy had taken a dislike to him.

In years to come Sammy and Susie would prove a huge visitor attraction. Fred would feed them every half-hour, on tiny pieces of fish, which they had to work for by leaping out of the water, propelling themselves up the ramp on their flippers, catching the fish in mid-air and generally doing 'tricks' which came naturally, and Fred's fingers would regularly get bitten by an overenthusiastic Sammy.

Charlie, our widower penguin, had died once his supply of herrings dried up early in the war. We had fed him on strips of horsemeat soaked in cod liver oil, but sadly his constitution couldn't cope with it. However, penguins are such extraordinary and popular birds that as soon as the herring situation improved, we got four new ones. Sadly a fox did for three of them, and Oswald – like Charlie – was left on his own. Also like Charlie – who had taken up residence with the remaining coypu after his companion had been killed by shrapnel – Oswald liked company and took to pushing his way through the fencing of his pen to go wandering.

If he timed it right he would meet Fred on his way to feed the sea lions. Ossie the ostrich would also lean over his fence as Fred passed and pinch pieces of fish from the bucket, while Fred would pretend he hadn't noticed. It was the same with the bears. Once they heard him coming, they'd stand on their hind legs and wave – as if to say, 'Hey, what about us?' So they too would get a bit of fish. Later the BBC filmed this happening and it made it into one of the short interludes they broadcast when there was a breakdown in transmission. Oswald took such a fancy to Fred that he would regularly follow him. One day Fred was up a ladder fixing some electrics in the reptile house when he felt something tugging on his trousers. He looked down and there was Charlie, eight feet off the ground, one rung behind him.

The arrival of the sea lions and their need for a large pool had far-reaching consequences. The cost of filling it with mains water, which needed to be constantly changed and replenished, was prohibitive, so Dad looked closer to home. Fortuitously, the first bore hole he drilled had gone straight into the centre of a huge aquifer. Once released, the water in this underground lake rose to the surface under its own pressure. Having filled the sea lions' pool, it coursed its way through filtration beds, along channels and down waterfalls, a weir and cascades, making pools wherever they were wanted – a flamingo pool, a beaver pool, a waterfowl lake. Not only did these waterways serve an important practical purpose in aerating the water, they added considerable visual interest and would eventually enable the construction of the lake that allowed the chimp islands to be built, as well as the canals which today make Chester Zoo unique in allowing visitors to see the zoo by boat.

It had taken me over eighteen months, but the aquarium was now stocked and ready. It held fourteen tropical tanks, eleven cold-water tanks and seven vivariums. As each cellar was a different shape, the route the visitor followed was a naturally winding one, going through each cellar in turn, passing tanks and vivariums of various sizes sunk into the cellar walls, where wine had once been stored. I had done what I could, but it took a great deal of looking after, as most things were makeshift. The snake pen, for example, had no trap and at feeding times it was a job stopping the large boa constrictor from swallowing the small royal python, who would persist in grabbing the boa's meal when he had already started to eat it.

While I was waiting for my fish to breed, I was also breeding parakeets. I made the nesting boxes out of wooden fruit crates, which I had great difficulty hanging firmly on the wall. I would know when youngsters had arrived when I heard them, but I'd have to wait until they left the boxes to find out how many there were, as there were no doors. But at last I was earning the zoo some money: Dad exchanged my surplus birds with Whipsnade for a camel.

The next urgent building project was an elephant house. When it was eventually opened, in late 1949, again by 'Nomad', he said, 'It looks, at a quick glance, to be a tolerable imitation of an old Greek temple.' It was built with the help of a crane and Molly herself.

Dad had managed to buy Molly from the owners. She had a decided character. While she would do anything for Kay, it wasn't the same for the rest of us, and we all treated her with the utmost respect. One of my jobs was helping the children up onto her howdah. She would delight in winding her trunk around my ankles as I stood on the top of the ramp to lift them on. I would be one side and Kay would be the other, and he would have a mischievous twinkle in his eye. I knew he wouldn't let me come to any harm, but even so, I would pray that she wouldn't pull me right off. Kay and Dorothy's daughter Nathalie was now about four years old, and Molly loved and protected her as if she was her own baby. Nathalie could run in between Molly's legs and do anything she liked with her, including demanding to be held aloft by her trunk.

One person Molly really took against was Fred. He supposed it was the smell of the bears. But whatever the reason, Fred was the enemy. Every evening Kay would bring Molly to the back yard, fix a hosepipe to the hot-water tap in the scullery and give her a bath. As the scullery was where the animals' food was prepared, it was hardly convenient, as everything had to stop. One day Fred got impatient – he was inside waiting to go out – so he made a dash for it. Molly lunged at him and he was caught between her head and the back wall. He said it was only because he'd been going down a steep step at the time that he wasn't crushed.

Every spring Molly had to get used to having the howdah put on. And once it was in place, she would try everything to get it off. Volunteers were needed so she could get used to the weight of someone sitting on her back. Although I never volunteered, I would usually get the job. She would go everywhere she knew would cause me trouble, walking under low-hanging trees, up close against brick walls. She would sit down, run, shake her head – anything to dislodge me – and all of this to Kay's obvious amusement.

Once she arrived at Chester Zoo, Molly was never shackled, but her sheer size frightened some of the smaller children so soon we were offering rides on donkeys and Shetland ponies as well.

During those years immediately after the war, holidays and even days off were rare. Everybody wanted to make the zoo a success. The cashiers would stay open as long as there was a chance of a couple of extra visitors turning up; the cafés were there to provide a service to the public and no matter how long a party lingered over their last cup of tea, we had to smile and be polite. The regular staff took great pride in the zoo. They worked long hours for very little pay. Their job satisfaction came with the knowledge that the zoo was expanding and the number of visitors increasing, and that they were part of it.

In 1949 the total number of visitors was 319,423 and 50,380 were prepared to pay extra for the aquarium, which I felt particularly proud of. The figures for the reptile house, built by Fred and Charlie Collins from war-surplus armoured glass and then run by Charlie as the keeper, had 102,613 visitors. As for the cafés, although my mother was still in charge, she now had a proper staff to help her. Looking at these figures now, it seems hardly credible what we had achieved. In 1949, 207,352 meals were served; 27,993 went for a motorboat trip round the Bird Island; 33,866 children had a donkey ride. As for Molly, she carried 30,350 people on her back.

After Muriel's discharge from the navy in 1945, she came home for a while, stayed long enough to bottle-feed a baby chimp called Pam, but then left again. She was still determined to travel and had got a job with Cunard as a stewardess on their ocean-going liners, including the *Georgic* and the *Franconia*, which had done service as a troop ship during the war, and finally the *Queen Eliza-*

beth. She went to Hong Kong and did the Atlantic crossing many times, to New York and Quebec. After a couple of years she'd had enough and returned to Oakfield. Her first love had always been the chimps, although sadly the group she had reared during the thirties did not survive the war years. Without sufficient warmth and a diet which was nothing like they needed to thrive, they simply got ill and died.

Dad was determined to build up a healthy chimpanzee colony, and with the help of Muriel, he did. In 1949 a doctor working in Sierra Leone gave the zoo five chimps of the western chimpanzee species. He had bought them at a local market, he said, where they had been offered for sale as food. When they arrived they were pathetic, undersized babies who would need love and care to survive. But thanks to Muriel and to Ziggy, who helped her and eventually took over as keeper, they became the ancestors of the chimps that are in the zoo today. One was Meg, the mother of the first chimpanzee ever to be born in captivity in Britain.

Muriel never shook off her wanderlust and after a few years looking after the chimps she emigrated to New Zealand, married and had a son, my nephew Robbie. Apart from one short visit home, she never returned.

Fred and I were married on 26 February

1949. I had always imagined that once the country was at peace, things would get easier, that rationing would end. It didn't. In fact it got worse. During the war at least bread was available. Now it too was rationed, we were told, to feed displaced people in British-occupied Germany.

If we wanted to hold our reception at Oakfield, Dad said, we'd have to choose a time when visitor numbers were at their lowest, which was why we waited until February. We were also limited as to the number of guests we could invite. Fred had seven brothers and their wives, and four sisters and their husbands or partners. I had all my aunties, uncles and cousins. And then there were our friends.

On the morning of the wedding, I got up early, took my net and went to collect daphnia from the pond, so I could give my fish a treat. Muriel cleaned and fed her chimps and then we got ready. I had a big bouquet which one of my soon-to-be sisters-in-law had made. I got dressed in my white gown (which I was entitled to wear) and veil, with a pretty wax orange-blossom headband. We had a minor panic, as Muriel had mislaid the new corset she had bought for the occasion. She looked so pretty in her rose-pink bridesmaid's dress. Fred's mum and my mum wore tweed suits, as it was February and really quite cold. Fred and his best man

Jim, his eldest brother, both wore smart new suits, each with a white carnation in the buttonhole. Dad gave me away.

For the reception, we had our usual ham salad, with tinned fruit and cream. Our wedding cake was beautiful, with three tiers, but there was no champagne to go with it, just a glass of sherry. None of our family drank, which was obviously a bit of a disappointment to Fred's, who definitely did. And the reason some of them aren't in the wedding photo outside the house is that they'd gone to the pub!

Our wedding presents included Pyrex dishes, dinner and tea services, two travelling blankets, a pressure cooker, an electric kettle, an iron, some table lamps and a very useful tray, which I still use today. They were already waiting for us in the lodge, which would be our home for the next five years.

Granddad was now bedridden. He had ulcers on his legs and needed dressings changed daily, and he had moved into one of the upstairs front bedrooms, overlooking the cedar tree – the one where the parrots used to roost – so that my mother could take care of him. But while his body was deteriorating, his mind, at ninety-three, was as sharp as ever.

The ceremony was at Upton Parish Church and when I got back to Oakfield, and before the reception, I went up to see him. I kissed him and shook the confetti that was still on me over him. He said he was very happy for us both.

Acknowledgements

I would like to thank all the people who made this book possible. Firstly my son George, whose idea it was and whose plan of the zoo's layout in the 1930s couldn't be better. Thanks are due also to Linda, my younger daughter, for my two grandchildren, who are a constant delight and whose intense interest in animals and wildlife reminds me of my younger days. Their great-grandfather would have been proud.

The lion's share of the praise, however, must go to my daughter Joy, who went through years and years of press cuttings and newsletters as well as my own notes and jottings, which she tirelessly sorted and typed out, photocopied, scanned and whatever else it's now possible to do. As I never filed anything systematically – and my handwriting would never have won prizes – this was not an easy task. She too was brought up in the zoo, and through her own clear memories of her grandfather and grandmother, who were important figures in her childhood, she was able to take me back in time. Her patience and generosity – she gave up a much-needed holiday to help me – have been incredible.

I would also like to thank my friend Nancy for her reminiscences of the war years, as well as my cousin Paddy and Fred's sister Jean for sharing what they remember.

Thanks too go to Adam Kemp who started the ball rolling, as well as all at Big Talk who turned our family's story into TV drama, especially Luke Alkin and Kenton Allen. And I will always remember the talented cast and crew who welcomed me so warmly into their family.

Thanks also to Sarah Emsley, Holly Harris and Juliana Foster at Headline, and Caroline Michel at PFD, for all their hard work and support. It could not have been easy. Many thanks too to Catherine Meredith for her hospitality.

Lastly I would like to thank Penelope Dening for her miraculous skill in putting it all together and bringing everything so vividly to life.

Picture Credits

The author and publishers are grateful to the following for permission to reproduce photographs:

Some of the photographs are from

Daily Herald/Science & Society Picture Library, Daily Mirror and Getty Images.

All other photographs from the author's personal collection.

Every effort has been made to fulfil requirements with regard to reproducing copyright material. The author and publisher will be glad to rectify any omissions at the earliest opportunity.

The publishers hope that this book has given you enjoyable reading. Large Print Books are especially designed to be as easy to see and hold as possible. If you wish a complete list of our books please ask at your local library or write directly to:

Magna Large Print Books
Magna House, Long Preston,
Skipton, North Yorkshire.
BD23 4ND

This Large Print Book, for people
who cannot read normal print,
is published under the auspices of

THE ULVERSCROFT FOUNDATION